ADVANCE PRAISE FOR

Portraits of Anti-racist Alternative Routes to Teaching in the U.S.

"Given the ongoing debate regarding alternative teacher preparation, Gist challenges traditional teacher preparation with exemplars of routes that have successfully recruited, prepared, and retained underrepresented teachers committed to social justice. For each route presented in the chapters, commentaries are uniquely provided to extend the conversation. This volume will assist teacher educators in developing a vision of new possibilities without compromising our commitment to educational and social justice."

—*Belinda Bustos Flores, PhD, Professor & Associate Dean of Professional Preparation, Assessment, & Accreditation, University of Texas at San Antonio*

"This is an enduring architectural digest that features structural innovations that support the entry of Teachers of Color to the profession. Critical teacher development that includes pillars—relational, intersectional and collective—makes this a timeless design for communities and teacher education visionaries."

—*La Vonne I. Neal, PhD, Associate Vice President & Professor, Northern Illinois University*

Portraits of Anti-racist Alternative Routes to Teaching in the U.S.

Rochelle Brock and Cynthia Dillard
Executive Editors

Vol. 104

The Black Studies and Critical Thinking series
is part of the Peter Lang Education list.
Every volume is peer reviewed and meets
the highest quality standards for content and production.

PETER LANG
New York • Bern • Frankfurt • Berlin
Brussels • Vienna • Oxford • Warsaw

Portraits of Anti-racist Alternative Routes to Teaching in the U.S.

Framing Teacher Development for Community, Justice, and Visionaries

Conra D. Gist, Editor

PETER LANG
New York • Bern • Frankfurt • Berlin
Brussels • Vienna • Oxford • Warsaw

Library of Congress Cataloging-in-Publication Data

Names: Gist, Conra D., editor.
Title: Portraits of anti-racist alternative routes to teaching in the U.S.:
framing teacher development for community, justice, and visionaries / edited by Conra D. Gist.
Description: New York: Peter Lang, 2017.
Series: Black studies and critical thinking; vol. 104 | ISSN 1947-5985
Includes bibliographical references.
Identifiers: 2017022493 | ISBN 978-1-4331-2789-2 (hardcover)
ISBN 978-1-4331-2788-5 (pbk: alk. paper) | ISBN 978-1-4331-4606-0 (ebook pdf)
ISBN 978-1-4331-4607-7 (epub) | ISBN 978-1-4331-4608-4 (mobi)
Subjects: LCS: Minority teachers—Recruiting—United States. |
Teachers—Alternative certification—United States. | Teachers—
Training of—United States. | Community and school—United States.
Classification: LCC LB2835.25.P67 | DDC 371.1—dc23
LC record available at https://lccn.loc.gov/2017022493
DOI 10.3726/b11418

Bibliographic information published by **Die Deutsche Nationalbibliothek.**
Die Deutsche Nationalbibliothek lists this publication in the "Deutsche Nationalbibliografie"; detailed bibliographic data are available on the Internet at http://dnb.d-nb.de/.

The paper in this book meets the guidelines for permanence and durability of the Committee on Production Guidelines for Book Longevity of the Council of Library Resources.

29 Broadway, 18th floor, New York, NY 10006
www.peterlang.com

Printed in the United States of America

being confident of this very thing, that He who has begun a good work
in you will complete *it* until the day of Jesus Christ
Philippians 1:6

Table of Contents

Illustrations

Tables

CHAPTER ONE

Teacher Development for Community, Justice and Visionaries

CONRA D. GIST

The preparation and development of teachers is contested terrain in the field of education. At stake is claim to who owns the right to license and develop teachers who will prepare future generations. As a consequence of this battle, the merits of alternative routes to teaching (ARTs)—characterized by troubling neoliberal policies and practices—are often sidelined, leaving possibilities for critical collaborative social justice work frequently overlooked. On the one hand you have neoliberal supporters highlighting research that asserts Teach for America (TFA) teachers, for example, are better at raising student achievement than traditionally prepared teachers (Clark, Chiang, McConnell, Sonnenfeld, & Erbe, 2013). On the other hand, you have critical researchers contending that although this appears to be a common sense line of inquiry, it represents the coalescing of increased private interest and competition (Lipman, 2002) and reduced government control and elitism (Kumashiro, 2010), all aligned to distort the work of justice by claiming to be vanguards of the New Civil Rights Movement (Duncan, 2009). Looking from the margins of the debate both sides appear stuck in a "dangerous dichotomy" (Grossman, McDonald, Hammerness, & Ronfeldt, 2008), and in the process, social justice alliances are weakened by the struggle. For one, the fact is alternative preparation programs are unlikely to be extinguished from the field of teacher education in the future. If critical researchers and scholars are to meet the challenge of reframing the dominant narrative towards the central issue of educational justice for marginalized youth in the United States, then we need a vision of what critical teacher development can look like, not simply a clear picture of what it is not. To address this issue, this book presents program portraits of what ARTs and professional development initiatives can look like when focused on recruiting and retaining Teachers of Color (i.e., Teachers who identify as Hispanic, Black, Asian/Pacific Islander, American Indian/Alaska Native, or multiple races). By featuring four distinct program initiatives, and the visions and designs that distinguish them, we can begin to better understand how alternative teacher development models for Teachers of Color can take shape.

ALTERNATIVES ROUTES TO TEACHING

Alternative certification is a narrowly defined term used to note policy regulations that allow for sidestepping traditional licensing protocols to offer quick entry to the teaching profession. Typically such permissions are granted to program initiatives that recruit aspiring teachers to enter the profession outside of the traditional teacher education program design and structure (Feistritzer, 2011). However, all ARTs are not reliant on alternative certification as a means to certify teachers. Zeichner and Hutchinson (2008) explain that traditionally ARTs have been defined as "anything other than a four-or-five year undergraduate program in a college or university, a definition that classifies college and university postbaccalaureate teacher-preparation programs as alternative" (p. 17). Further, they note, "the choice between a traditional program and an alternative route is not a choice between some professional preparation and no such preparation, but rather a decision about the timing and institutional context for teacher preparation and the mix of professional knowledge and skills to be acquired" (p. 19).

Grossman and Loeb (2008) explain ARTs by differentiating between program models depending on the philosophy/mission, providers, recruitment and selection, labor market needs addressed, and timing and focus of preparation. This conceptual framing offers a useful interpretation of how all teacher development models can be conceived and executed across a range of models. Scholars and policymakers must more closely analyze the motives and outcomes associated with ARTs to understand how they address teacher shortages as well as their philosophical and justice commitments related to the mission and design of educator preparation and teacher development. Of particular interest in this volume are programs that take a critical stance on schools and communities by viewing them from strength-based perspectives, positioning education as a social reconstructivist vehicle for individual and collective agency, and advocate and/or advance strategies, coalitions, and practices that challenge broader systems of structural racism that rely on unjust power relations and social inequality.

CRITICAL TEACHER DEVELOPMENT

To anchor our conceptual understandings of various philosophical and practitioner orientations guiding the design of teacher development models, Feiman-Nemser (2011) provides an overview of the following teaching and learning orientations: technological (i.e., achieving developmental performance indicators), practical (i.e., ability to apply knowledge of teaching and learning in practice), personal (i.e., humanistic and agency approach to learning), critical (i.e., teacher as activist), and academic (i.e., deep content knowledge of the disciplines). This conceptual framework is useful for not only understanding traditional teacher education programs, but also teacher development models in general. Although Feiman-Nemser (2011) is clear that these are not exclusive categories, and at times the orientations are prioritized differently depending on a teacher's stage in the program, it is clear the critical orientations toward teaching and learning can significantly distinguish the design of the program. Thus, in this volume I am specifically concerned with programs and initiatives that have such critical dimensions, in order to a) identify structures that define them, b) focus the goals of teacher development on cultivating critically conscious Teachers of Color, and c) consider implications for ARTs committed to justice, communities, and visionaries.

Gist, Flores, and Claeys (2014) explain critical teacher development "as a socio-constructivist process in which teachers work as change agents in knowledge-centered communities of practice that assess, implement, and refine rigorous and culturally responsive pedagogy to increase achievement for all students" (p. 19). We further go on to explain,

> We view teachers of color as critical assets for redefining effective teaching for culturally and linguistically diverse students, and as such, draw from their historical and emerging knowledge systems and instructional practices to develop the Critical Teacher Development Theory. Therefore, this theory challenges teacher education and professional development programs to employ teaching and learning methods that integrate teachers' cultural, linguistic and instructional knowledge systems. Thoughtful and targeted focus on non-dominant perspectives at each stage of the teacher development continuum (e.g., recruitment, preparation, retention, induction, and ongoing professional development) can equip teachers of color to be advocates for social justice in schools. (p. 20)

Such preparation encompasses particular philosophical groundings, understandings, and approaches for justice in communities and schools. Feiman-Nemser (2011) argues critical orientations position the teacher as "educator and political activist" (p. 88), and yet "it is easier to visualize the kind of teaching that supporters reject than the kind of teaching they can seek to promote through teacher preparation. The discourse about critically oriented teacher preparation is quite often theoretical, and practices to achieve particular purpose have not been clearly articulated" (p. 88). Yet, recent scholarship has been begun to advance our vision for what is possible.

Arellano, Cintron, Flores, and Berta-Avila (2016) assert the importance of preparing teachers who can: advocate for a social justice perspective across school, community, and political contexts; use and further develop students' cultural funds of knowledge, bilingualism, and biliteracy; lead students to achieve academically high standards across the core curriculum; guide students to explore issues of prejudice, discrimination, and multiple forms of oppression involving people of different races, socioeconomic classes, language varieties, abilities and disabilities, and sexual orientation; and promote school transformation toward equity and social justice on multiple levels (p. 41). They also explain that the Grow Your Own Teacher Education Institute (GYO-TEI) signature courses, aimed at preparing the next generation of Latino and Latina Grow Your Own Teachers, requires teaching topics such as: a social justice paradigm; naming and interrogating practices and policies in public schools; critical race theory; critical pedagogy; socio-cultural teaching/learning theory; language, literacy and culture; and a creative praxes (p. 42).

Delgado Bernal and Aleman (2017), in their work on educational pathways for Chicana/o students in their ten-year partnership with Adelante, emphasize the importance of "recast[ing] university-school-community partnerships as reciprocal, subversive, and enduring projects…these partnerships rarely attempt to destabilize racist structures while prioritizing the needs of marginalized communities, nor do they infuse equity and social justice work in sustainable and comprehensive ways" (pp. 5–6). In this sense, there is a need for school and university partnerships, including teacher development models to explicitly address racism. Zygmunt and Clark (2016) set forth a vision of social justice in teacher education by offering a vision about what this work can look like in an educator preparation program. The community teacher, critically prepared and trained, can address racism. Their framing of the development of community teachers involves the following: learning from community members, critical service learning and community mobilization, inviting community expertise, developing agency and taking action, community voices, and promoting social justice. Sleeter (2013) outlines philosophical and praxis implications for multicultural teacher education, similar to the focus espoused by Arellano et al. (2016), as potentially including some combination of critical pedagogy, critical race theory, and anti-racist education. With respect to teacher education for social justice in particular, she argues the importance of preparing teachers to provide equitable access to high quality, intellectually rich, culturally affirming teaching; foster democratic engagement among children and youth; and be equity advocates for children and youth. These approaches and conceptual frameworks for teacher development also extend to the preparation of

Teachers of Color through recruitment and admission, professional coursework, and guided fieldwork.

Collectively, this literature highlights the possible content, pedagogies, philosophies, and goals that can drive teacher development models committed to the critical teaching and learning orientations (noted by Feiman-Nemser, 2011) in clear and explicit ways. Grounded in this recent critical teacher education literature, I argue programs guided by critical teacher development for Teachers of Color should encompass some combination of the following attributes:

1. Develop anti-racist educational structures that support the recruitment and retention of Teachers of Color
2. Create and employ responsive and tailored preparation practices that address the philosophical and praxis teaching and learning needs and strengths of Teachers of Color
3. Provide advocacy, organizing, and justice vehicles for Teachers of Color to identify challenge, and restructure power relations and social inequality in schools and neighborhood communities
4. View and position local community partnerships and leadership as integral and vital to the program mission, impact and long-term sustainability

The explicit naming of critical teacher development for Teachers of Color is vital because of the strengths and value they can potentially bring to the profession: (1) they serve as role models, improve student academic outcomes, and desire to teach in hard to staff schools (Villegas & Irvine, 2010); (2) have high expectations, knowledge of community and ethics of care (Michie, 2011); and (3) have commitments to racial and social justice (Achinstein & Ogawa, 2011; Kohli, 2012). Yet, structural barriers to the recruitment and retention of Teachers of Color have been extensively documented in the literature and begin well before they enroll in college (Villegas & Davis, 2007). The poor K-12 schooling conditions (Valenzuela, 1999); unqualified and/or unresponsive educators (Grissom & Redding, 2016); meager socioeconomic opportunities (Villanueva, 1993); deficit/normalizing curriculum (Salinas & Castro, 2010); institutional racism in the policies and practices of schools (Morris, 2016); and dissonance between home and neighborhood community experiences and schooling culture (Moll & Arnot-Hopffer, 2005) are just a few of the systemic issues that restrict Teachers of Color. These barriers can coalesce to create a broader system of structural racism that extend to the higher education and teacher preparation classrooms, limiting access and opportunity for students of color to enter the teaching profession.

Given these barriers, there must be structural inventions in place to support the entry of Teachers of Color to the profession. This requires addressing race and racism along the teacher development continuum via social/cohort groups

(Bennett, Cole, & Thompson, 2000); persistence strategies/mechanisms (Bouck, 2012); scholarships (Lau, Dandy, & Hoffman, 2007); advocating for alternative certification exam practices and policies (Petchauer, 2014); mentorships (Jones & Jenkins, 2012); culturally responsive and tailored curriculum (Clark & Flores, 2001); field work experiences that explicitly address race and racism (Rogers-Ard, Knaus, Epstein, & Mayfield, 2012); partnerships with school districts to support hiring and retention (Ware, 2012); loan forgiveness (Podolsky & Kini, 2016); and responsive professional development and leadership supports (Kohli, 2012). Structural interventions, in particular initiatives such as Grow Your Own Programs, have also been developed to recruit Teachers of Color from nontraditional backgrounds and pipelines to the profession (Skinner, Garreton, & Schulz, 2011). These pools of Teachers of Color typically include high school students, paraprofessionals, parents, community activists, and/or college educated mid-career changers who are from the community and interested in staying in the community (Toshalis, 2014). Although there has been increased interest in developing these types of program models, we still know little about how these teachers impact schools and persist in the profession (Sleeter & Milner, 2011). What remains most important, however, is on the one hand, recognizing the challenges Teachers of Color face, and on the other hand, making explicit commitments to insert structural program interventions to confront and dismantle these challenges. A critical teacher development framework for Teachers of Color holds teacher education programs and practitioners accountable for such commitments.

Community, justice, and visionaries

In order to offer more conceptual depth to the idea of critical teacher development for Teachers of Color beyond the four attributes I outlined (i.e., develop structures, responsive and tailored preparation, vehicles to restructure power relations and social inequality, and community partnerships and leadership), it is helpful to briefly explore how critical teacher development is linked with commitments to community, justice, and visionaries. In a chapter focused on interrogating critical pedagogy and Teachers of Color (Gist, 2014b), I argue "constructs for change, such as community and justice, present useful opportunities for framing a critical stance or position, as well as, articulating a set of actions" (p. 56). I note,

> Collins' (2010) explication of community as a political construct is useful based on her citation of the following potentialities: (a) Community provides a template for relational thinking and social theories that strive to understand these relations; (b) it has a track record as an adaptable, functional principle of social organization; (c) it is associated with symbolic boundary construction; and (d) can serve as a template for aspirational projects. In light of the distinctive social and symbolic properties of community as an ideological

> tool, how can teachers of color utilize community as a political tool to address issues of essentialism, mobilization and identity stratification? (p. 56)

Community as a construct for change addresses and is interwoven into all four attributes of Critical Teacher Development in that it is relational, intersectional, collective, and possesses organizational potential to work toward justice for communities who need them most by challenging structural obstacles. In other words, critical teacher development is grounded in a identity and stance focused on collective, yet nuanced and complex, aspirations concerned with disrupting inequality through the justice acts of teachers. In the same chapter on interrogating critical pedagogy for Teachers of Color, I also utilized Adams, Bell, and Griffin (2007) to explain social justice as a construct, noting,

> the goal of social justice education is to enable people to develop the critical analytical tools necessary to understand oppression and their own socialization within oppressive systems, and to develop agency and capacity to interpret and change oppressive patterns and behaviors in themselves and the institutions and communities of which they are a part. (p. 2)

Mobilized in community and grounded in clear understandings of social justice, the work of visionaries can be cultivated. Miller and Kirkland (2010), also cited in that same chapter on interrogating critical pedagogy and Teachers of Color, offer a more humanistic vision of social justice, rationalizing,

> if social injustice deposits pain, then social justice is a process of healing wounds caused by social conflict (Kirkland & Filipiak, 2008)—a process of depositing hope as cure and inventing change as remedy. It is also the custodial work of repairing a broken world, a dangerous world that in many ways promises that people—all people—at some point in their lives will sustain wounds. (p. 4)

Seeing the world in its brokenness, and having the heart and resolve to engage in such "custodial work" of healing, in my view, requires seeing beyond what the eye can see. Seeing beyond the brokenness to the possibility of wholeness. This is the work of visionaries. In an analysis of a 2013 Woodson Lecture given by Dr. Kaye Wise Whitehead, I explain that justice can be viewed as "a spiritual epistemology that frames humanity as potential reconcilers for what is right in an immoral world" (Gist, 2014a, p. 29). I further assert,

> Submitting to justice, humans commit to service, acting as "living sacrifices" who stay on course by "pressing forward for the mark of the high calling." The Woodson Lecture awakens a deep spiritual connectivity through a moral imperative. Simultaneously, the battle cry also articulates a clear set of conscious-raising behaviors—shifting narratives, sparking genius, and learning how to see beyond—that concretize humanity's obligatory relationship with justice. (p. 30)

This vision of justice involves molding and cultivating visionaries possessing a vision of what can one day be. I further argue this could mean,

> seeing the day when the erasure of the achievement gap is realized; the provision of equitable funding across schools and resources is enforced; and a critically engaged and informed citizenry in local school communities work collectively to improve the quality of their lives. If teachers are to lead students, they must have a vision of a world where justice reigns. Perhaps in this sense, grading papers, recommending students for advanced placement, calling parents, late night curriculum planning, early morning tutorials, and Saturday professional development sessions, can all to be viewed as opportunities to perform justice by working towards what is right. Then, these are not a list of duties in the job description of a teacher, instead, they can quite possibly be individual subversive acts for justice that may make a child's life better, or increase their chances of realizing dreams they are scared to dream. Teachers are no longer problems to be solved but visionaries who model the work of justice. Imagine a society where teachers are a critical mass of mathematicians, scientists, writers, historians, and theorists who fight for justice in the classroom each day. In the face of stories of inadequacy that dominate schooling discourse, the justice worker may not only be required to see beyond, but also to believe justice is an attainable goal. (p. 32)

Interweaving a set of tight knit justice, community, and vision commitments infuses a soul in critical teacher development that reaches past hallow attempts at rigorous teacher training without a deep abiding purpose. Instead of grasping for what has consistently evaded us, applying critical teacher development for Teachers of Color, as a potential aspirational community in solidarity, positions them to utilize education to powerfully transform society in ways that enable all of humanity to live (and have access to) just and actualized lives. It is these types of visions that must drive our understanding of critical teacher development, and the types of ARTs we imagine for Teachers of Color.

BOOK OVERVIEW

Although scholarship has described programs that address the experiences of Teachers of Color (Ball & Tyson, 2011; Gist, 2014c; Orelus & Brock, 2014; Sleeter & Milner, 2011; Sleeter, Neal, & Kumishiro, 2014), the framing of ARTs that take place and/or originate outside the context of traditional teacher education programs, with a critical teacher development focus, is limited in the literature. Thus, the vision for this book is to create possibilities for reimagining teacher development from a critical stance. And the need for critical, transgressive voices from the margin, whether in the form of programs, scholars or policies/practices, always abound. For example, Ladson-Billings (2005) describes the unique and necessary role African American teacher educators play in the "big house" as they negotiate the privilege and responsibility of working in the academy. Their insider/

outsider knowledge speaks to the important disruptive and critical role they must play, but also revealed the structures that at times prevent teacher education from becoming a liberatory and transgressive space. Thus, the need for faculty of color in teacher education programs is not merely an argument about representation, but also about the need for alternative perspectives, views of knowledge, structures, narratives and discourses, and strategies for reimagining traditional teacher education spaces.

A central question this book seeks to grapple with, therefore, is *how can ARTs be framed, developed, and executed from critical perspectives that work to challenge and dismantle systems of oppression for Teachers of Color?* In order to answer this question, this volume spotlights program initiatives that, while not perfect or flawless, have innovative and relevant frameworks and strategies for contributing to our current understandings of how ARTs can be utilized to recruit and retain Teachers of Color. The program initiatives represent seeds of possibility for creating teaching and learning models grounded in critical teacher development.

Program Selection

As our nation prepares to replace 1.9 million teachers over the next decade in kindergarten through postsecondary classrooms, a critical mass of teachers will come from ARTs (Vilorio, 2016). To ensure the next generation of teachers are poised to teach in schools and communities fractured by inequality and oppression, we need critical teacher development models executed by visionaries who use constructs of community and justice in praxis to reimagine educational possibilities for a more democratic society. This book project endeavors to make such a contribution to the field by collecting, organizing, and portraying attempts of such critical social justice efforts in ARTs in hopes of lighting a path for other justice seekers to follow. Each program portrait is followed by a brief commentary from a scholar in the field to "talk back" to the program portraits and consider implications for the field.

Before presenting the program portraits, it is important to briefly explain a few methodological decisions that guided the organization of this book. First, this book features programs that create and/or support ARTs for Teachers of Color. They each, in different ways, represent interventions to the current structure and function of traditional teacher education programs. Hence, the program selection requirement for this book project were teacher development programs that did not originate from within traditional teacher education programs, but were the result of partnerships and/or goals explicitly aimed at addressing the needs of Teachers of Color because the structures in place at the higher education institution, school district, and/or local school community were inadequate. All four program initiatives have a critical teaching and learning orientation (as defined by Feiman-Nemser, 2011) in that Teachers of Color are positioned as educator and activist.

I examined current reviews and programs focused on Teachers of Color, coupled with my knowledge of programs engaging in this work, and developed a Call for Papers to solicit program portraits about their efforts to recruit and retain Teachers of Color. I sent an invitation to develop a chapter submission to the four program initiatives included in this book. Since this is a solo edited project, the decision was made to emphasize depth over breath in terms of the number of programs included for analysis. Also, although one of the programs is a professional development initiative (ITOC), it does represent an alternative teacher development model to support Teachers of Color post graduation. Given current research on the need for these types of supports to ensure the retention of Teachers of Color (Albert Shanker Institute, 2015), the decision was made to include this program initiative as a type of post-gradation alternative teacher development model to offer a more robust picture of the types of retention supports available for Teachers of Color.

The table below outlines the programs included, recruitment pool, program provider, and funding source.

Table 1.1. Overview of ART Programs and Professional Development Initiatives.

Program	Recruitment Pool	Program Provider	Funding Source
Teach Tomorrow Oakland (TTO)	College graduates from local community	School district	Federal grants and school district funds
California Mini-Corps Program (CMC)	Migrant bilingual college students	School district	Federal grant
Grow Your Own Illinois (GYO)	Mostly college students from nontraditional backgrounds	Non-profit organization	State allocated funds and private foundations
Institute for Teachers of Color Committed to Racial Justice (ITOC)	Classroom teachers connected to social justice and community organizing networks	University department	University and conference fees

Portrait Development Process

The writing of program portraits was a methodological tool chosen to spotlight the key structure framing each program in order to paint dynamic pictures of each initiative. Each program portrait also begins with a description of an image or picture that encapsulates the vision and focus of the program. This methodology stands in contrast, for example, to a positivist research paradigm, which is often characterized by the veneer of rigor, but lacks contextual depth and is unable to answer the why and how questions that are fundamental to understanding a phenomenon in the fullness of its complexity. In this sense, this book project represents a humble search for goodness (Lawrence-Lightfoot & Davis, 1997) to identify ARTs that are committed to fighting the good fight of justice for Teachers of Color. Although some would argue having an outside researcher conduct case studies and develop portraits would address concerns regarding subjectivity in relation to validity, the use of an outside researcher does not in itself resolve the inherent subjectivities that all observers of a phenomenon bring to their interpretations. In this case, having at least one program director who is intimately involved in the execution and development of these programs write the program portrait offered a window of insight that would have been more difficult to obtain as an outside observer. Also, to challenge the silencing of participant voices that can take place in positivist designs, this approach honors the people on the ground as the scriptwriters of their own experiences (Delgado Bernal, Burciaga, & Flores Carmona, 2012).

In order to support the development of the program portrait, each writer was given a protocol to structure the chapter focus and offered two rounds of feedback to refine their descriptions of the work and adhere to the objective of the book project. Scholars with expertise related to each program portrait were recruited to read the chapter and develop commentary about the program in general, and the implications for teacher development in particular, in an effort to triangulate interpretations of the programs. This also helped to substantiate validity since commentary for each program portrait was developed by at least one full professor with expertise in teacher education. Once the program portrait and commentaries were complete, I conducted a cross-analysis of the portraits using the four components of critical teacher development for Teachers of Color (i.e., develop structures, responsive and tailored preparation, vehicles to restructure power relations and social inequality, and community partnerships and leadership) to make sense of the structures, goals, and understandings that shaped the work of the programs.

Chapter Overview

The first program portrait featured in chapter two is Teach Tomorrow in Oakland, a local community based initiative launched by the Oakland Unified School District to recruit and retain more Teachers of Color. This chapter is immediately followed by commentary written by Drs. Militz-Frielink and Neal that contemplates the program from an endarkened feminist perspective and considers implications for ARTs that unwittingly subscribe to privatizing and deprofessionalizing teacher education. The California Mini-Corps Program is then described in the third chapter, as a partnership between federal, state, university, and school districts to bring more Teachers of Color from migrant worker backgrounds into local school community classrooms. Commentary developed by Dr. Flores immediately follows this chapter grappling with the potential for expanding nontraditional pipelines for teaching in the future. Next, the fourth chapter describes the GYO Illinois Program, a community-based effort to recruit parents, paraprofessionals, and activists to be teachers in their local school communities. Commentary for this program chapter by Dr. Michelli explores lessons learned with respect to recruiting and retaining Teachers of Color as well as considers areas where additional research is needed. The fifth chapter describes the Institute for Teachers of Color (ITOC) Committed to Racial Justice, a critical race theory guided intensive professional development program, to demonstrate how Teachers of Color can be positioned as racial justice leaders in urban schools. Program commentary developed by Dr. Villegas for this chapter points to possible implications for traditional teacher education programs concerned with increasing the number of Teachers of Color entering their programs. The book then concludes with a chapter using the critical teacher development framework to engage in a cross analysis of programs and explore themes related to structures and supports needed for ART Teachers of Color.

Finally, I must note that throughout this book the term Teachers of Color is capitalized to acknowledge their collective history and give credence to more contemporary efforts to view group standpoints from a perspective of solidarity to create equitable and engaging educational opportunities. Teacher of Color share sociopolitical histories of marginalization by education institutions, structures, policies, and practices, as well as transformative pedagogical and resistant community based practices, which is why they are often positioned from a group standpoint when theorizing and conducting research because it affords more comprehensive and complex understandings of their experiences (Dilworth & Brown, 2008).

REFERENCES

Adams, M., Bell, L. A., & Griffin, P. (2007). *Teaching for diversity and social justice* (2nd ed.). New York: Routledge.

Achinstein, B., & Ogawa, R.T. (2011). *Change(d) agents: new teachers of color in urban schools.* New York: Teachers College Press.

Albert Shanker Institute. (2015). *The state of teacher diversity in American education.* Retrieved from http://www.shankerinstitute.org/sites/shanker/files/The%20State%20Teacher%20Diversity%20Exec%20Summary_0.pdf

Arellano, A., Cintron, J., Flores, B., & Berta-Avila, M. (2016). Teaching for critical consciousness: Topics, themes, frameworks, and instructional activities. In A. Valenzuela (Ed.), *Growing critically conscious teachers: A social justice curriculum for educators of Latino/a youth* (pp. 39–66). New York: Teachers College Press.

Ball, A. F., & Tyson, C. A. (Eds.). (2011). *Studying diversity in teacher education.* Lanhma, MD: Rowman & Littlefield.

Bennett, C., Cole, D., & Thompson, J. (2000). Preparing teachers of color at a predominately White university: A case study of project team. *Teaching and Teacher Education, 16*(4), 445–464.

Bouck, G. M. (2012). The role of social capital in student persistence and retention in career pathways: A theoretical framework. In K. E. Jenlink (Ed.), *Teacher preparation in career pathways: The future of America's teacher pipeline* (pp. 125–142). Lanham, MD: Rowman & Littlefield.

Clark, E. R., & Flores, B. B. (2001). Who am I? The social construction of ethnic identity and self-perception in Latino preservice teachers. *Urban Review, 33*(2), 69–86.

Clark, M. A., Chiang, H. S., McConnell, S., Sonnenfeld, K., & Erbe, A. (2013). *The effectiveness of secondary math teachers from Teach for America and the teaching fellows programs executive summary.* Retrieved from https://ies.ed.gov/ncee/pubs/20134015/pdf/20134016.pdf

Collins, P. H. (2010). The new politics of community. *American Sociological Review, 75*(1), 7–30.

Delgado Bernal, D., & Aleman, E. Jr. (2017). *Transforming educational pathways for Chicana/o students.* New York: Teachers College Press.

Delgado Bernal, D., Burciaga, R., & Flores Carmona, J. (2012). Chicana/Latina testimonies: Mapping the methodological, pedagogical, and political. *Equity & Excellence in Education, 45*(3), 363–372.

Dilworth, M. F., & Brown, A. L. (2008). Teachers of color: Quality and effective teachers one way or another. In M. Cochran-Smith, S. Feiman-Nemser, & D. J. McIntyre (Eds.), *Handbook of research in teacher education: Enduring questions in changing contexts* (pp. 424–444). New York: Routledge.

Duncan, A. (2009). *Secretary Arne Duncan Speaks at the 91st Annual Meeting of the American Council on Education.* Retrieved from https://www2.ed.gov/news/speeches/2009/02/02092009.html

Feiman-Nemser, S. (2011). *Teachers as learners.* Cambridge, MA: Harvard Education Press.

Feistritzer, C. E. (2011). *Profile of Teachers in the US, 2011.* Washington, D.C.: National Center for Education Information.

Gist, C. D. (2014a). A call to action: Teaching for social justice. In K. W. Whitehead, *Sparking the genius: The 2013 Woodson lecture* (pp. 29–37). Baltimore, MD: Apprentice House Publisher.

Gist, C. D. (2014b). Interrogating critical pedagogy: Teachers of color and the unfinished project of justice. In P. Orelus & R. Brock (Eds.), *Interrogating critical pedagogy: The voices of educators of color in the movement* (pp. 46–59). New York: Routledge.

Gist, C. D. (2014c). *Preparing teachers of color to teach: Culturally responsive teacher education in theory and practice.* New York: Palgrave Macmillan.

Gist, C. D., Flores, B. B., & Claeys, L. (2014). A competing theory of change: Critical teacher development. In C. Sleeter, L. I. Neal, & K. K. Kumashiro (Eds.), *Addressing the demographic imperative: Recruiting, preparing, and retaining a diverse and highly effective teaching force* (pp. 19–31). New York: Routledge.

Grissom, J. A., & Redding, C. (2016). Discretion and disproportionality: Explaining the underrepresentation of high-achieving students of color in gifted programs. *AERA Open, 2*(1), 1–25.

Grossman, P. L., & Loeb, S. (Eds.). (2008). *Alternative routes to teaching: Mapping the new landscape of teacher education.* Cambridge, MA: Harvard Education Press.

Grossman, P. L., McDonald, M., Hammerness, K., & Ronfeldt, M. (2008). Dismantling dichotomies in teacher education. In M. Cochran-Smith, S. Feiman-Nemser, & D. J. McIntyre (Eds.), *Handbook of research on teacher education: Enduring questions in changing contexts* (pp. 243–248). New York: Routledge.

Jones, R., & Jenkins, A. (2012). *Call me mister: The re-emergence of African American male teachers in South Carolina.* Charleston, SC: Advantage Media Group.

Kohli, R. (2012). Racial pedagogy of the oppressed: Critical interracial dialogue for teachers of color. *Equity and Excellence in Education, 45*(1), 181–196.

Kumashiro, K. K. (2010). Seeing the bigger picture: Troubling movements to end teacher education. *Journal of Teacher Education, 61*(1–2), 56–65.

Ladson-Billings, G. (2005). *Beyond the big house: African American educators on teacher education.* New York: Teachers College Press.

Lau, K. F., Dandy, E. B., & Hoffman, L. (2007). The pathways program: A model for increasing the number of teachers of color. *Teacher Education Quarterly, 34*(3), 27–40.

Lawrence-Lightfoot, S., & Davis, J. H. (1997). *The art and science of portraiture.* San Francisco, CA: Jossey-Bass.

Lipman, P. (2002). Making the global city, making inequality: The political economy and cultural politics of Chicago school policy. *American Educational Research Journal, 39*(2), 379–419.

Michie, G. (2011). "I went to this school…I sat in your seat": Teachers of color as change agents in city schools. In E.A. Skinner, M.T. Garreton, & B.D. Schultz (2011). *Grow Your Own Teachers: Grassroots Change for Teacher Education. Teaching for Social Justice* (pp. 104–118). New York: Teachers College Press.

Miller, sj, & Kirkland, D. (2010). *Change matter: Critical essays on moving social justice research from theory to policy.* New York: Peter Lang.

Moll, L. C., & Arnot-Hopffer, E. (2005). Sociocultural competence in teacher education. *Journal of Teacher Education, 56*(3), 242–247.

Morris, M. W. (2016). *Pushout: The criminalization of Black girls in schools.* New York: The New Press.

Orelus, P., & Brock, R. (Eds.). (2014). *Interrogating critical pedagogy: The voices of educators of color in the movement.* New York: Routledge.

Petchauer, E. (2014). Slaying ghosts in the room: Identity contingencies, teacher licensure testing events, and African American preservice teachers. *Teachers College Record, 116*(7), 1–40.

Podolsky, A., & Kini, T. (2016). *How effective are loan forgiveness and service scholarships for recruiting teachers?* Retrieved from https://learningpolicyinstitute.org/product/how-effective-are-loan-forgiveness-and-service-scholarships-recruiting-teachers

Rogers-Ard, R., Knaus, C. B., Epstein, K. K., & Mayfield, K. (2012). Racial diversity sounds nice; Systems transformation? Not so much: Developing urban teachers of color. *Urban Education, 48*(3), 451–479.

Salinas, C., & Castro, A. (2010). Disrupting the official curriculum: Cultural biography and the curriculum decision making of Latino preservice teachers. *Theory and Research in Social Education, 38*(3), 428–463.

Skinner, E. A., Garreton, M. T., & Schultz, B. D. (2011). *Grow your own teachers: Grassroots change for teacher education. Teaching for Social Justice.* New York: Teachers College Press.

Sleeter, C. (2013). *Power, teaching, and teacher education: Confronting injustice with critical research and action.* New York: Peter Lang.

Sleeter, C., & Milner, H. R. (2011). Researching successful efforts in teacher education to diversify teachers. In A. F. Ball & C. A. Tyson (Eds.), *Studying diversity in teacher education* (pp. 81–104). New York: Rowman & Littlefield.

Sleeter, C., Neal, L. I., & Kumashiro, K.K. (2014). *Diversifying the teacher workforce: Preparing and retaining highly effective teachers.* New York: Routledge.

Toshalis, E. (2014). Grow your own teachers for urban education. In H. R. Milner & K. Lomotey (Eds.), *Handbook of urban education* (pp. 217–238). New York: Routledge.

Valenzuela, A. (1999). *Subtractive schooling: Issues of caring in education of US-Mexican youth.* Albany, NY: State University of New York Press.

Villanueva, V. Jr. (1993). *Bootstraps: From an American academic of color.* Urbana, IL: National Council of Teachers of English.

Villegas, A. M., & Davis, D. (2007). Approaches to diversifying the teaching force: Attending to issues of recruitment, preparation and retention. *Teacher Education Quarterly, 34*(4), 137–147.

Villegas, A. M., & Irvine, J. J. (2010). Diversifying the teaching force: An examination of major arguments. *The Urban Review, 42*(3), 175–192.

Vilorio, D. (2016). *Teaching for a living.* Retrieved from https://www.bls.gov/careeroutlook/2016/article/education-jobs-teaching-for-a-living.htm#by-the-numbers

Ware, M. L. (2012). Infect your own: Delaware's ASPIRE—Academic support program inspiring renaissance educators. In K. E. Jenlink (Ed.), *Teacher preparation in career pathways: The future of America's teacher pipeline* (pp. 49–63). Lanham, MD: Rowman & Littlefield.

Zeichner, K., & Hutchinson, E. A. (2008). The development of alternative certification policies and programs in the United States. In P. Grossman & S. Loeb (Eds.), *Alternative routes to teaching: Mapping the new landscape of teacher education* (pp. 15–29). Cambridge, MA: Harvard Education Press.

Zygmunt, E., & Clark, P. (2016). *Transforming teacher education for social justice.* New York: Teachers College Press.

CHAPTER TWO

Teach Tomorrow in Oakland: Combating Cultural Isolation and Revolving Doors for Teachers of Color

RACHELLE ROGERS-ARD

Figure 2.1. Teach Tomorrow in Oakland Symbol.
Source: Teach Tomorrow in Oakland Organization

Our symbol reflects the notion of promise: we can help you reach your goal to become a teacher.

Table 2.1. Teach Tomorrow in Oakland (TTO) Program Overview.

Funding Source and Period	Transition to Teach federal program 2009–2014 Transition to Teach federal program 2011–2016 Oakland Unified School District 1 2009–2015
Mission	To recruit and retain local, permanent teachers who reflect the diversity of Oakland students.
Timing of Preparation and Support	Varies depending on applicant and extends beyond initial entry into the classroom
Partnerships	Holy Names University, National University, California State University East Bay
Teacher Retention Rate	We define retention as teachers who complete their five-year commitment as a teacher in our district. As of 2015, 73% of all teachers were on track to complete five years; 42% had already completed three or more years, and 22% had completed seven years.

HISTORICAL OVERVIEW

Oakland, California has long been the site of radical racist struggle, reformation, and reform. Prior to World War II, Blacks constituted 3% of the population; after the war, there was an influx of Blacks and Latinos to work in the shipyards and on the railroads (Spencer, 2005). Oakland experienced the first "white flight" when more than 100,000 white property owners left Oakland for neighboring suburbs between 1950 and 1960. By 1966, only 16 of the city's 661 police officers were black (Spencer, 2005). Numerous expressions of racial struggle, especially between the police and Oakland's inhabitants of color allowed the manifestation of the Black Panther Party along with other groups designed to disrupt systems of oppression within the city of Oakland. Fifty years later, racial strife continues to be a huge part of Oakland as with many urban cities. Oakland has a diverse constituency: the hills have predominantly white inhabitants, while "the flats" are where disenfranchised groups, mainly Latino and Black, live and navigate. This same pattern is true for the schools in Oakland; the "hills" schools are predominantly white, and the flatland schools are often populated by Black and Latino students with families in poverty. This is the sociopolitical context in which a new program for Teachers of Color was formed.

Teach Tomorrow in Oakland (TTO) was created in the midst of citywide turmoil over the outsourcing of relatively good paying teaching jobs to National recruiting partners, which left local candidates unable to gain employment. Mayor Ronald Dellums called for community members to engage around several issues, one of which was education (Sleeter, Neal, & Kumashiro, 2014). Our community recognized the need to create an anti-racist program to interrupt the teaching reservation system designed for whites (Epstein, 2005). Therefore, TTO would recruit, develop and retain local Teachers of Color who would commit to teaching in Oakland's schools for at least five years. The program began in 2008 as a district-based initiative that grew with federal Transition to Teach funding, and was extremely timely because Oakland Unified School District had begun outsourcing its recruitment efforts while under state takeover. This reliance on National partnerships, such as Teach for America and The New Teacher Project, created a revolving door (Rogers-Ard, Knaus, Epstein, & Mayfield, 2012) where teachers were coming in and out of classrooms with little connection to the local community and its students.

In addition to the local focus, TTO was created to ensure that recruitment efforts were targeted towards teachers who represented the diversity of Oakland's children. Researchers have documented the value of having an increasingly diverse teaching force: Teachers of Color act as role models for children of color; teachers from similar backgrounds can often reach their students in ways outsiders could not; and local teachers from the community are more likely to be retained (Branch, 2001; Epstein, 2005, 2006; Sleeter, & Milner, 2011).

However, although we agree that we need more Teachers of Color we have not moved very far in producing them. Gordon (1994) documented the need for recruiting large numbers of diverse teachers 23 years ago, yet 84% of our nation's teachers are white and 71% of those are white women. Approximately 2% of the nation's teachers are African American men (Mitchell, 2016). Meanwhile, 48% of our nation's children are of color and by 2050, 62% of our nation's children will be of color (DeMonte, 2013).

Our teaching workforce demographics raise critical issues about who and what we value as holders and disseminators of knowledge. If we value young, white, female teachers as the pinnacle of excellent education, we will continue to recruit teachers from elite Universities to serve for a couple of years in our nation's poorest schools. However, if we value community leaders and parents as the first, authentic teachers; local residents who share similar backgrounds and cultures as our children and teachers from diverse cultural backgrounds as educators, we will shift resources to ensure candidates of color can push through the barriers in place—the traditional "teaching reservation system for whites" (Epstein, 2005)—and develop and implement alternative strategies and approaches to diversify the teacher workforce.

TTO TEACHERS: REACH AND TEACH

The racial divide I outlined in the introduction provides an interesting context for the recruitment and retention of effective teachers. Those who desire to teach in Oakland must be able to influence and reach students in both the hills and the flatlands schools. While it is a mistake to assume that all prospective teachers who share a child's race will share the child's experience, many times there can be an affinity between a person who looks like the child or members of his/her family that can create a bond with that child and a sense of authenticity with their families. The crux of our recruitment, then, must be recruiting and selecting local teachers who reflect the diversity of Oakland's children and who will engage in anti-racist pedagogical strategies. To ensure this takes place TTO purposefully utilizes a "reach and teach" philosophy for our teachers. For prospective Oakland teachers, we are far more interested in the person actually reaching children by creating safe classroom environments, developing relationships with each child, embedding the culture of each child into the classroom, and using multiple culturally relevant pedagogies to ensure the child's engagement. Once a child is engaged—or has been "reached"—learning can begin. It is the ability to utilize best classroom practices in the midst of an ever-changing curricular environment that helped convince us it was our job to adequately recruit and prepare teachers for Oakland. In order to foster teachers who actualize this model our work encompasses five phases that support TTO teachers: recruit, select, induct, place, and retain.

TTO RECRUITMENT: A NON-TRADITIONAL APPROACH

At its core, TTO holds the belief that teachers are *made* not hired, which is why TTO uses non-traditional recruitment strategies (i.e. partnering with faith-based organizations, non-profits, and other groups who work with and reach under-represented groups, as a practice). TTO then creates individual plans for each prospective teacher, including test-prep, assistance with enrollment in credential programs, and other needed supports towards removing pre-service barriers. It is important to note that TTO is not an alternative certification agency; it is a district-based program that uses alternative certification to ensure that recruits have an entryway into the profession. In California, prospective teachers who choose to utilize alternative routes to certification are interns who teach full-time as teachers of record, draw a full-time salary with benefits, and complete their preliminary credential during evenings and weekends. Alternative certification is the way in which a majority of Teachers of Color enter the profession; the traditional student-teaching route, which forces candidates to work for free for one year is not appealing to many Teachers of Color who are head of household and cannot afford such privilege (Epstein, 2006; Humphrey & Weschsler, 2007; Rogers-Ard et al., 2012; Shen, 1997). However, alternative certification is not enough to diversify the teaching workforce; ***we must reframe the way in which we think about exactly who we recruit into our schools and place in front of our children.***

TTO: Confronting the Problem

RECRUIT	SELECT	INDUCT	PLACE	RETAIN
Culture of Equity = PERSONALIZED SUPPORTS				
➢ Targeted marketing ➢ Monthly recruiting sessions	➢ Interviews ➢ Teaching demo. ➢ Program acceptance	➢ Spring Six-Week training ➢ Summer PD: 3 week intensive "boot camp" ➢ Testing Prep & Support	➢ Interview Prep ➢ Portfolio & resume development ➢ Placement support	➢ Classroom Supplies ➢ Monthly PD ➢ PLCs ➢ Mentoring towards leadership

Figure 2.2. Teach Tomorrow in Oakland Teacher Development Continuum.
Source: Teach Tomorrow in Oakland Organization

Many teachers prepared within traditional university programs do not come into the classroom prepared for Oakland's unique historical context, as demonstrated by high turnover rates at our neediest schools. While University curricula is rich in theoretical concepts that are designed to garner a basic understanding of the foundational concepts of education, urban schools districts need teachers who are ready to reach and teach children from the very first day. Therefore, if the university-based teacher education programs do not adequately prepare new teachers to understand students' social and economic context or give teachers the tools needed to be effective within that context—whose job is it? One of our Principals recently commented, "Everyone can teach, but not everyone can teach *here*" (personal communication, 2016). Again, Oakland is a city rooted in oppression, but is also a city focused on principles of revolution, critical discourse, and engagement. Teaching in Oakland is a revolutionary act, one that is based in historical roots and one that needs consistent support. Consequently, our work became more about continuous support in the form of professional development than recruitment. No longer can we assume that universities, with their overwhelmingly white, male faculty (Kena, Hussar, McFarland, de Brey, Musu-Gillette, Wang, Zhang, Rathbun, Wilkinson-Flicker, Diliberti, Barmer, Bullock Mann, & Dunlop Velez, 2016) will adequately prepare prospective teachers to reach and teach children at our hardest to staff schools.

We are convinced that no one knows how best to reach and teach Oakland's children more than current effective Oakland teachers who represent the city's diversity. Our local theory borrows heavily from Placed-Based Education (PBE), which is a teaching strategy focused on using the local community to teach subjects across the curriculum (Gruenewald & Smith, 2014; Smith, 2002; Sobel, 2004). Placed-Based Education deepens students' connections to community, fosters understanding of the local context outside of the classroom, and places students' needs at the forefront of the curriculum. While PBE focuses on using environmental studies as a way to engage students, the notion of finding meaning through activities within the local context and applying those strategies to problem solving resonates with the work TTO is doing because we believe teachers who are rooted in our community will remain in the classroom, reach our students, and ultimately, gain greater student outcomes.

TTO SELECTION: A COMMUNITY PROCESS

> *I'm tired of all these cute, white teachers who don't know what to do with our children. I'm tired of having to teach all of the black boys and black girls. I'm tired of having to explain their family dynamics to other teachers. And I'm real, real tired of having to hold up blackness for everyone else to see—who am I, Oprah?*
>
> —PERSONAL COMMUNICATION, 2015

Our reliance on PBE strategies is seen most heavily through our selection process, which is rigorous, but is also based on our local context. Once prospective teachers have demonstrated the ability to move forward with supports in the program (i.e. participating in tutoring, enrolling in a credential program) we ask candidates to teach a lesson in front of children from our current teachers' classrooms and the local Boys and Girls clubs. We also invite current TTO teachers, Principals, and community members to observe candidates' teaching demonstrations. All observers use a rubric to determine if the candidate would be good for Oakland's community. For adult observers, we are looking for evidence that candidates can relate to children, are not afraid of children, and can quickly develop a rapport within a classroom setting. However, one of the questions on the children's rubric is "is this a good teacher for your school?" versus "is this a good teacher?" because we believe children are extremely intelligent and astute, and they know which teachers will be successful in highly traumatized contexts. So, we ask if the candidate would be good at their school to personalize the process.

The notion of having the community participate in the selection criteria for teachers who will be working in their context is purposefully done. We use Anti-Racist Pedagogy (Schick & St Denis, 2003; Wagner, 2005) in our work by positioning the community to name and frame racism as well as engage in the process of owning and bringing value to educational experiences. Having prospective Teachers of Color observed and evaluated by students, teachers and community members who look like them is helpful and, for some, affirming of the work they want to do. Further, it allows community input that provides ownership of the candidates, which in turn gives the hiring manager (who is often new to the school) a "stamp of approval" when a candidate is placed at the site. This process is critical in a district like Oakland, where relationships are highly valued and the educational need is so acute. Centering student and community voice allows for dialogue, partnership and underscores the notion that TTO and district staff should not be the determining factor when placing prospective teachers at a school site. Parents, staff, students, and community members should own the process.

TTO UNIVERSITY PARTNERSHIPS: CHALLENGES AND POSSIBILITIES

While our selection process is rooted in community ownership, we are not a credentialing agency so it is imperative that we have deep partnerships with local universities. Using best practices by programs at California State University Long Beach and California State University Dominquez Hills, and in an effort to deepen our partnership with local universities, we proposed allowing district personnel to teach methods courses and suggested meeting regularly with local universities to share what was happening in the district. We were met with resistance from certain Universities; one University program actually told us they would not "cross the bridge" to work with interns. Another program indicated they would come to meetings only if the district paid for their participation. However, we were able to identify one private university with which we still have a deep partnership. Holy Names University allows candidates to enroll and take some coursework before passing the state subject-matter competency test, has rolling admissions so candidates can begin in any one of four quarters, and TTO coaches and university supervisors work together to ensure curricular alignment when coaching district interns.

While Holy Names University was by far the institution most willing to shift policies to ensure the success of their students, not every TTO teacher can afford to attend Holy Names, which is a private University and one of the most expensive programs in the surrounding area. This meant that some teachers received a great deal of support, and others faltered, necessitating the need for more aligned, consistent district support.

TTO INDUCTION: COMBATTING CULTURAL ISOLATION

> *Everytime an angry Black parent comes in, my Principal asks me about it. She always wants to know, "Did I handle that right?" "Would you mind talking to him/her?" As if I'm the ambassador to Black people everywhere. Just because I'm the only one on this campus doesn't mean that I represent all Black people.*
>
> —PERSONAL COMMUNICATION, 2014

> *On any given day, I'll have 5 – 7 little black boys in the back of my room…other teachers' students! Just because I'm the only black teacher on site, they send all of the black boys to me. What I want to know is when they will learn how to teach these boys instead of sending them to me everyday?*
>
> —PERSONAL COMMUNICATION, 2012

Our program began with preservice support that allowed new and prospective teachers to be deeply immersed in the strategies needed to be successful at the beginning of their journey. We felt this gave teachers the advantage of working with current, effective classroom instructors who are familiar with Oakland's unique context. However, we began to notice another phenomenon: 60 years past Brown vs. the Board of Education, we were still asking people of color to desegregate school site faculty. Our recruitment efforts yielded people of color but their placement at school sites often meant they became, through no fault of their own, the "one" or the "only" at the school site. It is up to us, as educational leaders, to create systems designed to support and retain Teachers of Color, especially those battling "cultural isolation." I first used this term to describe the crippling trauma experienced by many of our Latino and African American teachers, particularly African American males, at school sites. While teaching is an act of resistance in Oakland's context, being the only African American male at a school site is polarizing and isolating.

What do educators of color find when they are placed at a school site? This question, not the original focus of our work, came as a result of conducting one-on-one interviews, listening during coaching sessions, having difficult conversations within small groups, and excavating nuggets of information when teachers discussed what bothered them at their school sites. Teachers often discuss low pay, lack of supplies, or even rough teaching conditions; those who choose to teach in the urban environment are aware of these conditions. But those items will not keep them from being retained because local teachers familiar with Oakland's context see these conditions as part of "the work." Many teachers discuss their administrators with a mixture of exasperation and respect—much the same way they discuss "the district"—but those larger systems do not keep them from teaching children. What can wear them down, however, is being the "one" or "only" on a campus and having few support structures in place to navigate those situations.

We have a tremendous amount of qualitative data outlining the journey of Teachers of Color who became the one or only at their school site, such as: (1) feeling they somehow had to be the representative for each and every child of color; (2) being asked to represent their entire race on every committee; (3) experiencing the fear of saying "no" when asked to take yet another African American or Latino boy to sit in the back of their class because the white teacher down the hall couldn't "handle" him; and (4) recognizing constant worry of "what happens after me?" The past six years have been filled with these stories. TTO teachers from Oakland, who have worked consistently on their craft and understand Oakland's context, are fearful for what happens when their children leave the academic and social-emotional safety of their classroom and regress when dealing with another, less capable teacher.

After listening to these repeating stories we began noticing a pattern. Those teachers who are most vocal about the disparate treatment children receive, those teachers who are most socially conscious and "awake" were often silenced through being reassigned, consolidated, or replaced. Some of the teachers who were most aware of the very context for which we prepared them were assigned to the portables at the back of the school site; in effect, removing them from professional school community in the same way teachers remove African American and Latino boys through suspension. For those who tried to play the game—remaining conscious but using the "I'm just going to teach in my own room" methodology—became extremely frustrated and looked for other teaching opportunities. One teacher left the district to teach in a charter school—even though the charter offered fewer health benefit and less pay because, as she explained, "They're asking me to teach things that don't make any sense for our children" (Personal communication, 2011).

It is imperative that school districts, especially urban school districts and those that serve large populations of color and children in poverty, must not reproduce "willful blindness" (Briscoe, 2015) when dealing with racist leadership and professional development methods for Teachers of Color. District administrators who avoid issues of racial marginalization (i.e., teachers' cultural isolation at school sites) must work on their own issues around race if they are be effective. Given that educational systems are inherently racist (i.e., designed to work for those for whom the system was designed) district leaders have to be extremely intentional in their desire to interrupt racist paradigms. When district leaders and administrators say, "we want to recruit more Teachers of Color," I often ask them, "what will they find when they get there? Are your systems in place to support more Teachers of Color?" This is where our work became less about recruitment, and more about retention—and for us, we define retention as the ability to give teachers the tools and strategies they need to be successful in Oakland so they will be able to remain for at least five years.

TTO PROFESSIONAL DEVELOPMENT

> *We recognize that the current education in the United States happily and vicariously silences indigenous people and other people of color, particularly those forced to live in poverty.*
>
> —(KNAUS & ROGERS-ARD, 2012)

Our Teach Tomorrow in Oakland program work over the past eight years surfaced a couple of key lessons: (1) teachers coming from traditional university credential programs were consistently unprepared for the Oakland context; (2) Teachers of Color with a critical social justice lens were often silenced and/or removed, and (3) all teachers need support, but teachers of color, who are often the "one" or "only" on a school site, need additional support battling cultural isolation. We responded to these lessons by becoming adept at providing that type of support for our teachers.

We began by offering monthly professional development sessions that were, at first, facilitated by district personnel. However, after reviewing data gathered during the first two years, it became apparent that Teachers of Color in Oakland's neediest schools needed more than traditional PD. Just as the program sought teachers with a socially conscious mindset, so did our PD need to be relevant and rooted in the local context. Who better to facilitate these sessions than our own teachers? Moving to a Teacher Leader model allowed for monthly sessions to be relevant and timely, provided opportunities for teachers to collaborate and design lessons, but also offered leadership and tiered support for teachers who were often taking on additional leadership roles at their school sites.

Because many of our newest teachers were taking classes to fulfill their credential on Saturdays, we also created "Tune Up Tuesdays" at various teachers' school sites, designed for teachers to collaborate after school around really specific lessons and designs with which they were grappling. While this was not as structured as the monthly PD sessions, teachers felt energized knowing they could drop in on Tuesdays if they needed additional help designing an assessment or using Google classroom, for example.

However, we are most proud of our response to intervention method by developing the "Men in the Classroom" affinity series. While the number of black males within TTO is larger than the national average of 2% (Mitchell, 2016), many of our male teachers were struggling to navigate a female-dominated profession while bringing their authentic voice to school sites where they were often the only male and/or the only male of color. We began offering the series every other month to ensure that all males, not just African American males, would have a safe place to share strategies for survival. The data coming out of that program was rich, dense, and deserves greater analysis. We believe bringing teachers together frequently to share best practices, navigate district policies, and create safe places to unpack racist educational ideology is reflected in our retention data, and thus, stops the flow of the revolving door.

TTO DISTRICT PARTNERSHIPS

Critical to TTO's success is the notion that *districts must frame and drive the training for its teachers, NOT university programs driven by accreditation demands*. The most important thing to remember about school districts, especially urban school districts, is that change is the norm. From schools to central office, change happens quickly and without much notice. If universities are not in lock step with those changes, they will not be able to adequately prepare candidates to be successful. University faculty must be willing to revise and adapt curricula, syllabi, and teaching techniques to reflect the standards being set in their neighboring districts. Further, university faculty must partner with district mentor or master teachers to ensure that new candidates are using the technology and strategies designed for teacher effectiveness.

Granted, universities often note that they cannot prepare students for just one district because they have no idea where their students might land. While this is true, it would also be helpful to group students in cohort classes by the districts and school contexts where they most want to work. In that way, universities concerned about diversifying the teaching workforce could create professional learning communities by district as a support system for alternative certification students to increase retention.

Still, universities cannot do it all. Districts also must take the responsibility to prepare teacher candidates and new teachers. While most states mandate that teachers follow a course of study designed to clear a preliminary credential, this is not helpful for the many teachers who are placed in classrooms through alternative certification. First, those teachers who are alternatively certified and earning their credential while teaching do not participate in state licensing programs. Second, teachers in alternative certification programs often need even more support, as they have a heavier load teaching every day and taking University courses at night and on weekends. Finally, numerous researchers question the effectiveness of such state mandates, especially since there is limited research clearly linking the impact university based teacher education programs have on teacher effectiveness (Feuer, Floden, Chudowsky, & Ahn, 2013) and teacher effectiveness itself is difficult to measure. TTO teachers liken those teacher education programs to "just another hoop and binder full of stuff" (Personal communication, 2012).

TTO'S PLACE-BASED TEACHER INDUCTION PROGRAM

Given these challenges of providing TOCs the opportunities they need, TTO advocates for a Place-Based Teacher Induction Program (PTIP) that includes two phases: pre-classroom service and placement towards tenure. Once applicants have been selected, a mandatory, rigorous pre-service program that meets state standards is held at the district for six weeks and is designed to match pre-service teachers with district-approved master teachers who will work with each teacher to design, craft, and outline the tools and methodology necessary to have a great beginning of school. It is imperative for the pre-service work to be aligned with state standards, and enable new teachers to receive credit towards earning their preliminary credential. These courses will allow new teachers to see alignment between university-based theory and classroom-based practice.

This is also a practical approach because the work happens during the last six weeks of summer break so Teacher Leaders can still enjoy vacation. Substitutes should also be required to attend these sessions; many hard-to-staff subject areas and schools are staffed with long-term subs at the beginning of school, and they need the same type of training as pre-service teachers. Teacher Leaders will ultimately serve as mentors and guides for a small group of teachers over the next two years during investiture (i.e., meetings held once monthly on Saturday mornings, 8:30 am – 1:30 pm; evenings are too difficult, and many new teachers are taking courses towards their preliminary credential during that time period). Too often, teachers are asked to attend numerous professional development sessions but not treated as professionals—not providing a decent place to meet, meals, and/or ensuring that the subject matter and work is relevant and aligned to their growth and development. Treating them, as professionals, will ensure their participation.

Inherent in the PTIP model is the understanding that one cannot be a Teacher Leader without having taught in the district for at least three years with evidence of exemplary teaching as designed by the district effectiveness rubric and observations and/or completion of the National Board Certification. Teachers who apply to be Teacher Leaders must demonstrate effective teaching techniques through classroom observations, high scores on the district's teacher evaluation tool, be reflective of the student population, have taught in some of our district's hardest to staff schools, and must have cleared their credential after entering the profession as an intern. This last requirement is critical and intentional; we understand that the majority of Teachers of Color are interns, and we want Teacher Leaders who understand the journey of an alternatively certified teacher to work with newly placed instructors.

Also critical to PTIP's success is the lens through which professional development is delivered. Using an anti-racist, critical race theoretical framework means that Teacher Leaders name and frame race—not just social justice—as the most important aspect of teaching. Social justice is usually a nice way of indicating that we want equity for all people, but TTO frames race as central to educational philosophy. Understanding the racial context of schools, the inherently racist paradigm on which all educational systems are designed, the relationship between race and power, and modeling the way to navigate those systems as a small percentage of the teacher population is critical to TTO teachers. This means that instruction and partnership must be delivered by critical pedagogues; those who are most adept at reaching and teaching our children through creating safe spaces for all children to thrive, learn and grow. Therefore, Teacher Leaders must be well-versed in anti-racist pedagogy, aware of the context and history of the district, master pedagogues in their classrooms, and committed to the growth and development of adults who are their colleagues. Selection for Teacher Leaders must be rigorous, and not just based on who people know. In addition to excellent scores on the effectiveness rubric, a video of teacher delivering instruction to their students that frames the way in which they handle difficult children and the multi-faceted layers within the local context is key to determining if the person would be an exemplar for new teachers.

In addition to the district-wide Professional Learning Communities offered to all teachers, the PTIP model allows for career ladders and professional development towards leadership for each Teacher Leader. It is imperative that each Teacher Leader is still in the classroom; we are not looking to pull wonderful teachers away from the classroom as Teachers on Special Assignment. Therefore, each Teacher Leader must understand adult learning theory and understand the need for their own individual development. Built into the structure are monthly leadership development courses that can be applied towards a Master's Degree or additional credit on the pay scale. In this way, the Teacher Leaders create their own Professional Learning Community, deepen their skills in the classroom and in leadership, help increase student achievement at their school sites, and ultimately, remain within the district. Since TTO has implemented the PTIP model we have a 76% retention rate of teachers over five years.

TTO FUNDING: NAVIGATING SUSTAINABILITY

Teachers are grown, not recruited; hire for the end result.

Our program was entirely funded through two federal Transition to Teach grants; only the Program Manager's position was a full-time position within the district. As funding ended, it became necessary to think of new and different ways to ensure that TTO best practices could continue. It quickly became apparent that our district did not have the additional resources necessary to support this type of model. Therefore, we are seeking out deep partnerships with community-based organizations that can support part of the work; for example, allowing the summer pre-service work to be held with a CBO, but holding the district accountable for setting up the structure for Teacher Leadership. However, funding will always be a challenge when seeking out the best possible way to develop teachers. It is up to us, educators across the nation, to influence policymakers so grant opportunities, and state-based funding is made available towards diversifying and creating a sustainable teacher workforce. Based on our qualitative and quantitative data, we know the TTO PTIP model is replicable, manageable, and measurable, and is the work educational policymakers should be funding.

REFERENCES

Branch, A. (2001). Increasing the numbers of teachers of color in K-12 public schools. *Educational Forum, 65*(3), 254–261.

Briscoe, F. (2015). A Counternarrative autoethography exploring school districts' role in reproducing racism: Willful blindness to racial inequities. *Teachers College Record, 117*, 080305.

DeMonte, J. (2013). High-Quality Professional Development for Teachers: Supporting Teacher Training to Improve Student Learning. Washington, D.C.: Center for American Progress.

Epstein, K. K. (2005). The whitening of the American teaching force: A problem of recruitment or a problem of racism? *Social Justice, 32*(3), 89–98.

Epstein, K. K. (2006). *A different view of Urban Schools: Civil rights, critical race theory, and unexplored realities*. New York, NY: Peter Lang.

Feuer, M. J., Floden, R. E., Chudowsky, N., & Ahn, J. (2013). *Evaluation of teacher preparation programs: Purposes, methods, and policy options*. Washington, DC: National Academy of Education.

Gordon, J. A. (1994). Why students of color are not entering teaching: Reflections from minority teachers. *Journal of Teacher Education, 45*(5), 346–353.

Gruenewald, D. A., & Smith, G. A. (Eds.). (2014). *Place-based education in the global age: Local diversity*. Routledge.

Humphrey, D., & Wechsler, M. (2007). Insights into alternative certification: Initial findings from a national study. *The Teachers College Record, 109*(3), 483–530.

Kena, G., Hussar W., McFarland J., de Brey C., Musu-Gillette, L., Wang, X., Zhang, J., Rathbun, A., Wilkinson-Flicker, S., Diliberti, M., Barmer, A., Bullock Mann, F., & Dunlop Velez, E. (2016).

The condition of education 2016 (NCES 2016–144). Washington, D.C.: U.S. Department of Education, National Center for Education Statistics. Retrieved from: http://files.eric.ed.gov/fulltext/ED565888.pdf

Knaus, C. B., & Rogers-Ard, R. (2012). Educational genocide: Examining the impact of national education policy on African American communities. *ECI Interdisciplinary Journal for Legal and Social Policy, 2*(1), 1.

Mitchell, C. (2016). *Black Male Teachers a Dwindling Demographic.* (2016, February 17). Retrieved from http://www.edweek.org/ew/articles/2016/02/17/black-male-teachers-a-dwindling-demographic.html

Rogers-Ard, R., Knaus, C. B., Epstein, K. K., & Mayfield, K. (2012). Racial diversity sounds nice; systems transformation? Not so much: Developing Urban Teachers of color. *Urban Education, 48*(3), 451–479.

Schick, C., & St Denis, V. (2003). What makes anti-racist pedagogy in teacher education difficult? Three popular ideological assumptions. *Alberta Journal of Educational Research, 49*(1), 55–69.

Shen, J. (1997). Has the alternative certification policy materialized its promise? A comparison between traditionally and alternatively certified teachers in public schools. *Educational Evaluation and Policy Analysis, 19*(3), 276–283.

Sleeter, C., & Milner, H.R. (2011). Researching successful efforts in teacher education to diversify teachers. In A.F. Ball & C.A. Tyson (Eds.), *Studying diversity in teacher education* (p. 81–104). New York, NY: Rowman & Littlefield.

Sleeter, C. E., Neal, L. I., & Kumashiro, K. K. (2014). *Diversifying the teacher workforce: Preparing and retaining highly effective teachers.* Routledge.

Smith, G. A. (2002). Place-based education. *Phi Delta Kappan, 83*(8), 584.

Sobel, D. (2004). Place-based education: Connecting classroom and community. *Nature and Listening, 4.* 1–7.

Spencer, R. C. (2005). Inside the panther revolution: The black freedom movement and the Black Panther party in Oakland, California. In J. Theoharis & K. Woodward (Eds.), *Groundwork: Local black freedom movements in America* (pp. 300–318). New York: NYU Press.

Wagner, A. E. (2005). Unsettling the academy: Working through the challenges of anti-racist pedagogy. *Race Ethnicity and Education, 8*(3), 261–275.

Teach Tomorrow in Oakland Commentary

LA VONNE I. NEAL AND SARAH MILITZ-FRIELINK

Our response to TTO Program Portrait is both data-informed and endarkened from the lenses of a senior scholar and an emerging scholar. This commentary is data-informed because we have analyzed the impact of neoliberal partnerships such as Teach for America and find them deficit in effective systemic solutions to systemic problems. Endarkened because we support Rogers-Ard's epistemology that "resituates research endeavors in their cultural and historical contexts—reclaiming their personal and social roots or origins" (Dillard, 2006, p. 17). As respondents to Rogers-Ard's chapter, which delivers a promising portrait of an established program alternative to neoliberal partnerships, we offer a commentary to spark broader considerations for racial and social justice in the field of teacher development.

TEACH FOR AMERICA AND NEOLIBERALISM

We use neoliberalism as an ideological lens to compare Teach for America (TFA) to the community-based program, Teach Tomorrow in Oakland, because TFA has been used to create and justify educational reforms and policies during the past three decades. We define neoliberalism as a:

> Political ideology which calls for state policies that better enable entrepreneurs to compete in the free market. Policies which promote privatization, deregulation, individual choice, and the reduction of government expenditures are valued over those which increase, or promote the welfare state and government control of social and economic activity. (Lahann & Reagan, 2011, p. 12)

Formed in 1990, TFA seeks to "build the movement to eliminate educational inequity" by recruiting "outstanding recent college graduates [who] teach for at least two years in urban and rural public schools" and continue to fight educational inequity beyond their two-year commitment through "strong leadership at all levels of the school system and every professional sector" (Teach for America as cited in Lahann & Reagan, 2011, p. 16).

Although data from some TFA studies has been positive (Xu, Hannaway, & Taylor, 2011), critics have contested their research methodology (Kovacs & Slate-Young, 2013). Additionally, decades of research studies have demonstrated that novice teachers trained through Teach for America programs have high-turnover rates and at times perform significantly less well in the classroom than their non-TFA counterparts (Darling-Hammond, 1994; Heilig & Jez, 2010; Laczko-Kerr & Berliner, 2002; Miner, 2010).

Our main contention is that we do not support the neoliberal assumption that predominantly white college graduates from elite universities who did not major in education are somehow better prepared to enter the classroom than licensed teachers trained in traditional teacher preparation programs at universities; especially teachers from the local community. Instead, we posit that TFA undermines public education's most spirited democratic values through "branding itself," and assuming that public education can best achieve educational equality through deregulation, forming public/private partnerships, and market reform.

In contrast to TFA, Rogers-Ard's portrait of Teach Tomorrow in Oakland (TTO) paints a completely different ideological picture. Based in an anti-racist, endarkened epistemology that recruits teachers who represent the diversity of Oakland's children, TTO believes that "teachers are made not hired." Data informs us that a diverse teaching force must thrive to promote "equitable educational policy decisions, student success, and to help disrupt degrading stereotypes and assumptions about marginalized groups" (Sleeter, Neal, & Kumashiro, 2014, p. 7).

Rogers-Ard shows us that some "university-based teacher education programs do not adequately prepare new [white] teachers to understand students' social and economic context or give teachers the tools needed to be effective within that contexts," and takes into consideration the historical and cultural context of Oakland as part of the TTO program. "Oakland is a city rooted in oppression, but is also a city focused on principles of revolution, critical discourse, and engagement."

Rogers-Ard skillfully illustrates how theories like Placed-Based Education and Anti-Racist Pedagogy breathe life into TTO—contributing to its success (as of 2015, 73% of TTO teachers were on track to complete in five years; 42% had already completed three or more years).

SITUATING TEACH FOR TOMORROW IN OAKLAND

Rogers-Ard's chapter compels us to remember the historical and contemporary struggles in Oakland, California. She takes us back to the "white flight" in Oakland during the 1950s and the endless expressions of racial strife, which mobilized the Black Panther Party along with other civil rights groups to push back against "systems of oppression within the city of Oakland." Then, Rogers-Ard takes us forward fifty years later when these conditions still remain with the white population dominating "the hills" of Oakland and the majority of Blacks and Latinos living and navigating in "the flats." Consequently, the neighborhood schools follow these same segregated patterns, often with the flatland schools populated by families of color and families in poverty.

So what does this mean for TTO? Until adequate numbers of Teachers of Color are hired in each urban school, the challenge of combatting cultural isolation when Teachers of Color find themselves being the only ones at a school site will remain. Ultimately, teachers in these urban school districts benefit from school administrators willing to proactively address the issues around race. Rogers-Ard outlines this painful reality and what it means for the lone TTO teacher of color in these urban placements, such as:

- Feeling they somehow had to be the representative for each and every child of color
- Being asked to represent their entire race on every committee
- Experiencing the fear of saying "no" when asking to take yet another African American or Latino boy to sit in the back of their class because the white teacher down the hall couldn't "handle" him
- Recognizing constant worry of "what happens after me?"

Nevertheless, we are not surprised as the systemic racism and segregation in Oakland continues to be a contemporary issue, even manifesting in the public eye. For example, in June 2016, the Oakland police department was transitioned to civilian control when multiple police chiefs stepped down during allegations of egregious misconduct by officers, such as the fact that during "…a 13-month period, looking at 28,000 field reports of stops, 17,000 of those stops involved officers halting black people on the street" (Quinlan, 2016, para 3).

Despite these harsh facts, we are invigorated by the endarkened tenets of TTO as the program continues to push past racial barriers and work with districts to "take responsibility to prepare teacher candidates and new teachers and not rely solely on the university." We recognize that systemic racism requires systemic change and that reform cannot come from a university partnership alone. TTO's grassroots approach pulls from many stakeholders and resources in the community including parents, staff, community members and teacher education programs.

Rogers-Ard gives us meaning and hope as she describes the Teacher Leaders in the TTO program who have taught in a district for three years, scored high on the district's teacher evaluation tool, earned their credentials and most importantly, can "name and frame race—not just social justice—as the most important aspect of teaching". We are encouraged by programs that focus on anti-racist paradigms that strive to deliver instruction through critical pedagogues—especially "those who are most adept at teaching our children through creating safe environments to thrive, learn and grow." This gives us pause for reflection and consideration for the future of teacher development programs in higher education and our communities at the local and national level.

ENDARKENED EPISTEMOLOGIES AND THE FUTURE OF TEACHER EDUCATION PROGRAMS

When we reflect on racial and social justice, and the future implications for teacher development programs at both the local and national level, we would like to see more programs like TTO and related plans and models, which are starting to diversify the existing teacher workforce (Sleeter et al., 2014). Looking onward to the development of new teacher preparation programs and community-based partnerships, we see promise in the possibility of endarkened epistemological-based educational policies.

For ideas, we look to Cynthia B. Dillard, who introduced endarkened feminist epistemology as a new research/teaching paradigm to the educational community at the American Educational Research Association Annual Meeting in 2000 (Dillard, 2006). Dillard, who is the Mary Frances Early Professor (endowed professor) and chair of the Educational Theory and Leadership Department at the University of Georgia, Athens is the author of *On spiritual strivings: Transforming an African American woman's academic life* (SUNY Press, 2006) and *Learning to (re) member the things we've learned to forget: Endarkened feminisms, spirituality and the sacred nature of research* (Peter Lang, 2012).

Along with black feminist thought (Collins, 1990); standpoint theory (Harding, 1987); the tenets of African American spirituality; and the work of

Parker J. Palmer (1983), Dillard has anchored her epistemology in the idea of being responsible for students' emotional and cultural safety and well-being. She explains:

> I want to engage a commitment to the spirit of community as the African spiritual mandate that it is, raising possibilities for rethinking teaching and research as spaces that are—or can become—deeply embedded in cultural memory and imbued with the intention of being responsible for the energy that we bring to the room as teachers and researchers. (Dillard, 2012, p. 84)

Dillard expressed her commitments to the Hippocratic Oath as an educator and strives to create a space in her classroom that "do no harm," which is very much in line with the way Teacher Leaders in TTO run their classrooms. She believed this was fundamental in helping students get to a place where they could understand social and racial justice. "The key is to protect them from injustice in the first place" (C.B. Dillard, personal communication, December 7, 2015). Dillard's pedagogy and epistemology helps address the systematic issue of racism that requires systematic change in our institutions. For example, she teaches at a predominantly white institution (PWI) and the majority of the students who register for her class are students of color. She asks us to critically consider two possibilities: (1) where are the places where there are explicitly no harm being done, particularly for black students in a PWI; and (2) if that possibility exists, then the other is the possibility to heal, and to heal through remembering who we are (C.B. Dillard, personal communication, April 14, 2016).

The fact that Dillard does not assume these conditions exist or take these conditions for granted is a wake up call for educators who still have work to do in creating a classroom that "does no harm" to students of color. While this is all too often a neglected element in higher education, we recognize that this charge should be a communal responsibility. Like Dillard, we answer the commitment to the spirit of the community and ask everyone who is directly or indirectly involved with the education of a human being (policy-makers, administrators, teachers, staff, parents, community makers) to be accountable for the energy they bring to the public spaces in education.

REFERENCES

Collins, P. H. (1990). *Black feminist thought: Knowledge, consciousness, and the politics of empowerment.* New York, NY: Routledge.

Darling-Hammond, L. (1994). Who will speak for the children? How "Teach for America" hurts urban schools and students. *Phi Delta Kappan, 76*(1), 21–34.

Dillard, C. B. (2006). *On Spiritual strivings: Transforming an African American's woman's academic life.* New York, NY: State University of New York Press.

Dillard, C. B. (2012). *Learning to (re)member: The things we've learned to forget.* New York, NY: Peter Lang.

Harding, S. (1987). *Feminism and methodology: Social science issues.* Bloomington: Indiana University Press.

Heilig, J. V., & Jez, S. J. (2010). Teach for America: A review of the evidence. *Education Policy Research Unit.* Boulder and Tempe: Education and the Public Interest Center & Education Policy Research Unit. Retrieved from: http://nepc.colorado.edu/files/PB-TeachAmerica-Heilig.pdf

Kovacs, P., & Slate-Young, E. (2013). Performance versus promises: An evaluation of Teach for America's research page: Executive summary. *University of Alabama Education Policy Center.* http://uaedpolicy.weebly.com/uploads/6/1/7/1/6171842/tfa-2_1.pdf

Laczko-Kerr, I., & Berliner, D. (2002). The effectiveness of "Teach for America" and other under-certified teachers. Education Policy Analysis Archives, 10, 37. Retrieved from: http://epaa.asu.edu/ojs/article/view/316

Lahann, R., & Reagan, E. M. (2011). Teach for America and the politics of progressive neoliberalism. *Teacher Education Quarterly, 38*(1), 7–27.

Miner, B. (2010). Looking past the spin: Teach for America. *Rethinking Schools Online, 24*(3). Retrieved from: http://rethinkingschools.aidcvt.com/archive/24_03/24_03_TFA.shtml

Palmer, P. (1983). *To know as we are known: Education as a spiritual journey.* San Francisco, CA: Harper.

Quinlan, C. (2016, June 16). Three chiefs in 9 days: Oakland police department in scandal meltdown. *Think Progress.* Retrieved from http://thinkprogress.org/justice/2016/06/18/3790121/oakland-police-scandal/

Sleeter, C. E., Neal, L. I., & Kumashiro, K. K. (2014). *Diversifying the teacher workforce: Preparing and retaining highly effective teachers.* New York: Routledge.

Xu, Z., Hannaway, J., & Taylor, C. (2011). Making a difference? The effects of Teach for America in high school. *Journal of Policy Analysis and Management, 30*(3), 447–469.

CHAPTER THREE

Former Children of Migrant Farmworkers: A "Secret" Pipeline for Growing Your Own Bilingual and Bicultural Teachers in California

REYES L. QUEZADA AND ERNESTO RUIZ

Figure 3.1. California Mini-Corps Symbol.
Source: California Mini-Corps Organization

Symbol description: This logo was taken from the Aztec hieroglyphics. Each of the four bars represents a different entity: community, parents/families, teachers, and schools (institutions of learning). In the middle is the migrant child. All these geometric lines center on the child and the importance of each entity in ensuring the success of the migrant child (M. Avila, personal communication, June 4, 2016). It is up to us as future educators to uphold its meaning by supporting migrant children and their families through a collaborative and supportive approach that starts with our schools and institutions of higher learning where they attend, the teachers that teach them daily, the communities they live in, and the support of their families. Ignoring the four bars of each entity can result in the academic failure if migrant children are not at the center.

Table 3.1. California Mini-Corps (CMC) Program Overview.

Funding Source and Period	The CMC receives its funding from the California Department of Education as a statewide set-aside program. These funds derive from the state's Migrant Education, Title I—Part C, federal allocation. The contract period begins July 1 and ends June 30 of each year and funding amount averages 6.7 to 7.1 million dollars annually. The CMC program is administered by Butte County Office of Education, located in Oroville, California. Its central administrative staff is located in Sacramento, California.
Mission	The CMC mission is to increase migrant student academic achievement through high quality tutorial services provided by a cadre of highly skilled full-time college tutors; and to develop a pipeline for well trained credentialed future bilingual educators.
Timing of Preparation and Support	The CMC recognizes that teacher recruitment and preparation needs to begin earlier than the traditional student teaching programs. The CMC recruits undergraduate, former migrant college students who demonstrate an interest in a teaching career or a related field. Training begins as soon as the Teacher Assistant (TA) is hired. TAs can work up to 20 hours per week. It includes at least six hours of professional development monthly on select topics that will improve their tutoring effectiveness. These include but are not limited to lesson planning, classroom management and instructional strategies in math, English language arts and English language development. The training is paired with on-going cognitive coaching from a college coordinator, and bi-monthly observations by their Master Teacher.

Partnerships	Over its long history, the CMC established a strong network of support that helped institutionalize the program on 22 college and university campuses statewide. There are also 20 Migrant Education regional offices and a multitude of school districts.
Teacher Retention Rate	The CMC traditionally tracks participants during their time in the program. Over the last five years, the CMC began collecting data on participant transition into student teaching programs and the type of credentialed earned; 60% of CMC Tutors received teaching credentials and 70% in credentials in multiple subject areas, bilingual/cross cultural, or ELD/ESL.

FIRST AUTHOR'S PERSONAL CMC NARRATIVE

Mini-Corps allows teacher candidates to perfect their craft in an environment that is not detrimental to student achievement. They are in the classroom 15 to 20 hours a week for four years, every day for 180 days, compared to a student teacher that has a two-week observation period in the classroom for a couple hours and then a two-week solo period. So when they step into the classroom as a teacher, students don't have an (inexperienced) first year teacher.

—Personal communication, 2013

I recall many a time having to wake up at 5:30 in the morning during weekends and during the summer while in school beginning in 7th grade, if not even earlier, all the way up to my first year of community college. I, along with my four brothers and three sisters, worked in a ranch in the hot desert of Imperial County in Southern California 40 miles north of the Mexican border where my father had been employed as a farmworker since the early 1960's. At times we picked tomatoes, onions or garlic, while other times we pitched watermelons into large semi-truck trailers. We all "graduated" into better field jobs—my sisters moved to working in the packing sheds, while we loaded tomato boxes from the field to trucks. As we grew older we would dig ditches or unplug water sprinklers getting soaking wet in below freezing weather during the winter. All this time we would be with older workers who were three times our age. I always wondered why our father had us do this at such an early age but we knew it was to help the family economically. Conversations and the "consejos" (advice) the older men, (including my father) would give us day in and day out was "stay in school and make something out of your life or you will become one of us."

Throughout high school and up to my second year at the local community college I knew I wanted to either go into the military or be a police officer; my three older brothers had similar aspirations. But then a close family friend from the ranch had been killed in Vietnam and that discouraged me going into the military. I decided to choose Administration of Justice as a career as I was pursuing becoming a police officer with my twin brother. In the spring semester of 1977 my community college counselor gave me a brochure about a program called the California Mini-Corps that provided summer employment working with migrant students throughout California. I applied, interviewed and got accepted. I still remember getting my congratulations letter from the Sacramento office. At the age of 18 getting a letter from Sacramento seemed so important. I thought everything came from the governor's office! I think my parents must have been so proud of me because I could see it in their eyes when I left for a one week training that summer to Chico State University over 500 miles away from our home. Our first meeting and orientation was with other college students throughout California who looked and had similar experiences just like me and my family. It was such an amazing and eye opening experience meeting other Latinos/as who were enrolled in many California State Universities (San Diego State, Chico State, Sacramento State) and from University of California (UC Berkeley, UC Santa Cruz, UC Los Angles). Just by being enrolled at those institutions I thought they were automatically smarter than me since I was coming from a community college.

At the end of the week's orientation of learning about lesson planning, teaching math, English as a Second Language, Physical Education, and many other content subjects, I was assigned to work at an elementary school for eight weeks in the migrant education summer school program in Lompoc, California. I was placed with a host family, the father a White man, was an engineer at Vandenberg Air force base, and the mother was a Latina instructional aide working in the same migrant summer school where I was placed. For eight weeks, as a Mini-Corps tutor, I saw the challenges many migrant students, as well as their parents, faced in and out of the classroom. I was a classroom aide at the local community college teaching English as a Second Language to many of the same parents whose children were at our school. The connections I had with the families and their students were so impactful as I saw my father, mother, brothers and sisters in the same light. We were all the same immigrants from Mexico whose parents left their farms and migrated their families to the United States in search of better opportunities for their children. That fall when I returned to my local community college I changed my major to Liberal Studies because I wanted to become a teacher. I believed I could have more of an impact on students and families by carrying a pencil and a pen than a pistol—my twin brother and next older brother did become police officers and are now retired. For the next four summers I continued to work in the Mini-Corps program. Each summer I worked both in the Indoor Education Program as well as in their Outdoor Education Program. I later became one of their summer Outdoor Education Team Leaders, and the College Coordinator for the Mini-Corps Program at the same Community College where I started. I worked as the Mini-Corps Program College Coordinator for thirteen years while at the same time earning two Masters Degrees, one advanced degree and my doctorate. It was the Mini-Corps program that nurtured me throughout my professional career as well as thousands of others who have similar stories since its inception in 1967. These people are now professors, administrators, superintendents, college presidents, and most importantly TEACHERS—who continue to serve the migrant students in California schools and across the nation.

SECOND AUTHOR'S PERSONAL CMC NARRATIVE

When my former boss, County Superintendent Don McNelis, asked if I might be interested in heading up the California Mini-Corps Program, I jumped at the opportunity. This would mean coming full circle in my professional career in education, since I started my teaching career with California Mini-Corps in Salinas, California during the summers of 1974 and 1975. During those summers I found my passion and my career niche. For me, working in the classroom and teaching migrant children was much more than a summer job, it was a calling! When I looked into the eyes of those thirty migrant students some 42 years ago, I saw my myself and the struggles I encountered when I was their age—the educational challenges that come with a migrant lifestyle, working in the fields to help support the family, moving from school to school, and not speaking English. I made a vow to myself that I would make a positive difference in their lives. While I did not possess a teaching credential at the time, my students all called me "maestro." They were excited that their "maestro" spoke Spanish, understood their migrant background and was studying at the University of California, Santa Cruz to become a teacher. I WAS THEIR ROLE MODEL. In me, and my fellow Mini-Corps Teacher Assistants, they saw the possibilities of going to college and having a career outside of the fields. While the UC Santa Cruz student teaching program immersed me in teaching and learning theory, my experience in California Mini-Corps grounded me in teaching practice needed to become a successful teacher. The Mini-Corps summer professional development institutes and guidance received from my master teacher taught me lesson planning, classroom management techniques, and instructional strategies for teaching migrant English learners.

In my position as the California Mini-Corps State Director before I retired, I witnessed almost daily, the power, influence and legacy of this program. In all my travels throughout the state, there was never a single visit, where I did not encounter a teacher, principal or superintendent who was not eager to share their Mini-Corps story. With huge smiles and big eyes they shared how the Mini-Corps program made a difference in their lives and profession. Principals mentored their current Mini-Corps Teacher Assistants with the goal of offering them teaching positions when they completed their student teaching. It was powerful to walk in classrooms and not be able to distinguish between the master teacher or the Mini-Corps Teacher Assistant.

CALIFORNIA'S ATTEMPT TO MEET THE TEACHER SHORTAGE

California is one of the states in the union that has the highest population and the most culturally and linguistically diverse students. If it were a nation, it would be the eighth leading economy in the world (KPBS, 2015). California became a state in 1850 and is considered a land full of beauty and opportunity with its mountainous regions and great desert areas, edged by the Pacific Ocean. Several population booms secured California's status as an agriculture, business, aircraft, and movie industry powerhouse. Thousands of people came to the "Golden State" from Southeast Asia, Mexico, and Central America from 1946 to 1960. Many still consider California as one of the most coveted states, with bragging rights of the largest population, encompassing a diversity of languages, and consisting of almost a one-third immigrant population (U.S. Census Bureau, 2016). The influx of immigrants from all over the world to California is ongoing and has brought a dynamic and vibrant student population into our schools and classrooms that are composed of mostly low-income students of color. This has created the need for educator preparation programs in California to rethink how to produce culturally proficient teachers for the multi-ethnic, multilingual, 21st century student population (Lindsey, Robins, & Terrell, 2009; Quezada, Lindsey & Lindsey, 2012; Quezada & Louque, 2004; Quezada, Rodríguez-Valls, & Lindsey, 2016).

Recent evidence from school district data indicates that teacher supply has not kept pace with the increased demand in California, particularly after the last recession of 2012 as many school districts struggle to hire enough teachers. The most recent publication of the California Teacher (April/May, 2016) entitled "Crisis in the classroom: California confronts teacher shortage—Poor working conditions, modest pay, and teacher bashing exact a toll" reports that California is at a 12 year low. Over the last decade teacher preparation programs saw a 76% drop in admissions application to their colleges of education. In mid October of 2015 there were more that 3,900 open teaching positions in California, even after a 25% increase in teacher hires in the 2014–2015 school year. California has experienced a shortage of qualified teachers, as low-income students of color and students with special needs are disproportionately impacted by the shortage. About twice as many students in high-minority schools, in comparison to low-minority, schools were being taught by a teacher on a waiver or permit (a teacher not yet even enrolled in a preparation program) as reported by California's educator equity plan, in 2013–14 (Darling-Hammond, Furger, Shields, & Leib, 2016). Therefore, developing creative teacher recruitment and retention programs to attract teachers, and in particular teachers of color, bilingual teachers, special needs teachers, and STEM teachers, is crucial if we are to meet the needs of our growing ethnic minority student population.

THE CALIFORNIA MINI-CORPS PROGRAM: SERVING CALIFORNIA'S MIGRANT STUDENT POPULATION

From its inception, the California Mini-Corps Program (CMC) has positively impacted the educational lives of thousands of migrant children and contributed to California's bilingual teacher workforce. The California Department of Education (2016) reports the student K-12 California population to be at 6,200,000 enrolled in 10,393 schools during the 2014–2015 school year; this includes Charter School student enrollment. Over 53% are Hispanic/Latino/a children, 8% Asian, 6% African American, and yet, over two-thirds of the 295,000 teachers in California are White (Non-Hispanic) (California Department of Education, 2016). In the 2014–2015 school year, there were approximately 1.392 million English learners, the majority of which are Latino students for who Spanish is their primary language (California Department of Education, 2016). The demographics for the children of migrant farmworkers is no different; in 2012–2013, 360, 279 migrant students were enrolled in schools and one out of every three migrant students in the United States lives in California (California Department of Education, 2016). Currently, there are over 112,000 migrant students (a majority who are Hispanic) attending California schools during the regular school year and most attend summer/intersession classes. These demographic conditions call for educators and policymakers to examine and turn to programs such as the CMC to address these future educational challenges. The CMC is a successful alternative early clinical teacher preservice model that can be readily replicated and implemented to serve similar student populations in other states.

ESTABLISHING A FUNDING PIPELINE FOR CMC

The creation of the federal Migrant Education and CMC program sprung from the 1960's War on Poverty initiative during President Johnson's administration. According to the Interstate Migrant Education Council, migrant families' needs and their children's "success rate is minimal in a society that has left them to fend for themselves" (Interstate Migrant Education Council, 1988, p. 5). In an effort to meet the needs of migrant families and their children, the federal government reauthorized the Elementary and Secondary Education Act of 1965 to improve the education of America's children from disadvantaged backgrounds. Based on federal guidelines it included those who were identified as socioeconomically poor, and specifically addressed the children of migrant workers under Title I Part of the legislation that formulated in 1966. This legislation authorized the Migrant Education Program (MEP) to provide formula grants to state education agencies for the express purpose of establishing or improving educational programs for the children of migrant workers. In the preliminary and current Guidance for Title I, Part C, Public Law 103–382, the U.S. Department of Education states the following:

> The general purpose of the MEP is to ensure that children of migrant workers have access to the same free, appropriate public education, including public preschool education, provided to other children. To achieve this purpose, the MEP helps state and local education agencies remove barriers to the school enrollment, attendance, and achievement of migrant children. (U.S. Department of Education, 2016)

The MEP is the main entity nationally for the provision of supplementary educational and related services to migrant children and their families. Their services are aligned with the accountability and performance legislation of the 1990s, particularly the Improving America's School's Act of 1994, Government Performance and Results Act of 1993, and the Public Schools Accountability Act of 1999. The MEP is aligned with accountability and performance legislation to help migrant students "at risk" of failing each state's educational content and performance standards (Butte County Office of Education, 2012; Quezada et al., 2016). Using federal migrant education funds, states are able to provide academic services, remedial and compensatory programs, bilingual and multicultural education, counseling and preschooling programs. The MEP is administered in all 50 states including Hawaii, Alaska, District of Columbia, and Puerto Rico (U.S. Department of Education, 2016).

LAUNCHING THE CALIFORNIA MINI-CORPS PROGRAM

In California, a small group of forward thinking educational leaders understood the challenges facing migrant children, especially a teaching force that was not prepared to meet the educational needs of culturally and diverse student populations. Fewer teachers understood or were sensitive to the needs and educational challenges facing students who moved with their parents to follow the crops within and across state borders. Additionally, while institutions of higher education (IHE) were beginning to see more students of color on their campuses, the teacher workforce in California remained mostly, if not, exclusively White.

It was these conditions that prompted these educators to seek solutions to address these educational challenges and that planted the seeds for a program that endures to this date. The CMC was established in 1967 and modeled after the Peace Corps program through an innovative partnership among the California Department of Education, Chico State University and the Butte County Office of Education. The program originally started as a summer school program where fourteen college students with a farm worker background were recruited to work as teacher assistants in migrant-student impacted summer schools. Over the next six years, the program expanded and proved to be a promising vehicle for graduating ex-migrant students who went on to pursue careers in education. In 1974, the CMC expanded to the regular school year. In 1976, the State Board of Education adopted the California Master Plan for Migrant Education and in it, institutionalized the California Mini-Corps program. Under the Master Plan, the program would recruit and provide specialized training to college students with a migrant background that would enable them to provide tutorial services to migrant students. These college students would also receive preparation to help them become future bilingual-bicultural teachers (Butte County Office of Education, 2012).

CALIFORNIA MINI-CORPS PROGRAM GOALS & RECRUITMENT PLAN

The California Department of Education (CDE) funds the Mini-Corps Program through an annual contract using federal Migrant Education, Title I Part C dollars. Throughout its 50 year history, this contract has been administered through the Butte County Office of Education (BCOE) who is responsible for meeting the contractual deliverables including hiring staff, professional development and provision of regular year and summer instructional services.

The CMC encompasses two major goals:

- To provide direct instructional services to increase migrant student academic achievement through a cadre of trained college tutors.
- To develop a cadre of future credentialed bilingual educators who will be better equipped to meet the educational needs of migrant students.

The CMC recognizes that teacher recruitment and preparation needs to begin earlier than the traditional student teaching programs. As such, the CMC recruits undergraduate students, preferably with a migrant background that demonstrate an interest in a teaching career or a related field. Prospective candidates complete an application that includes an autobiography and reference letters. The local Mini-Corps College Coordinator whom administers the program at the institution of higher education where the program is located and housed then interview student candidates who met the program requirements. Once a candidate is hired, s/he participates in a comprehensive professional development program delivered through monthly all day workshops and a three day intensive summer institute. This educational training involved being paired with a Master Teacher on a bi-weekly basis to learn under his/her tutelage. The CMC tutors receive written feedback after each visit and observation from the Master Teacher. The CMC Master teacher also completes a comprehensive semester end evaluation of the assigned tutor. In addition, the supervising College Coordinator uses cognitive coaching strategies and questions to guide self-reflection and continuous learning to improve tutor instruction. Aside from the formal training and observations from Master Teachers, College Coordinators mentor tutors throughout their tenure with CMC. This mentoring includes guidance on college course selection, monitoring grades, preparation for teacher certification exams, building effective relationships with master teachers and developing a professional portfolio. This professional development and mentoring is one of the key elements to helping CMC college tutors successfully complete their undergraduate degrees, transition into student teaching programs, and eventually earn their teacher certification.

CALIFORNIA MINI-CORPS EXPANSION AND INSTITUTIONAL PARTNERS

Institutional partnerships are essential to CMC's success. The figure below illustrates this integral relationship. Over the last fifty years, the CMC has expanded to 22 community colleges and state universities (See Figure 3.2). The CMC formalizes their partnerships with the colleges and regional migrant education programs through memoranda of understanding. These agreements outline responsibilities for each agency, establishes in-kind services and ensures that partnering organizations demonstrate institutional buy-in and "ownership" for the CMC on their campuses and regions. In the state university programs, the CMC is often, if not always, an integral part of the school of education. Several regional migrant programs purchase additional tutor slots to augment their service delivery for migrant students. This alone speaks to the value regional partners place on the CMC and their tutors.

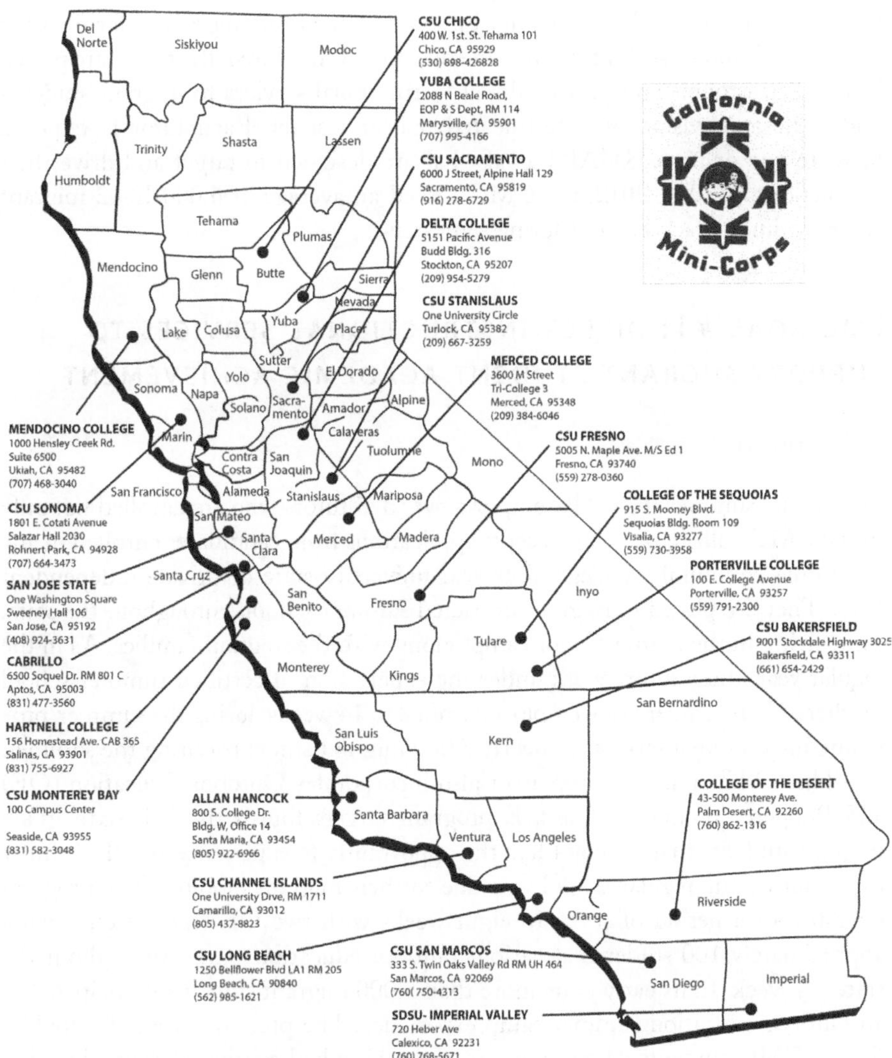

Figure 3.2. California Mini-Corps Project Sites.

RECRUITMENT OF TUTORS FOR SCHOOL YEAR PROGRAM

Currently, the program provides tutorial support to K-12 migrant students during the regular year and summer school. During the regular year, each project site is staffed by a certified project coordinator, a part time office assistant, and employs 18–25 college bilingual tutors, averaging 450 total tutors for the school year at any given time. To be eligible to work as a MC tutor, applicants must be full-time undergraduate college students, bilingual, come from migrant or farmworker background, and be seeking a career in education. Once hired, the tutors are placed in K-12 classrooms and provide direct instructional services to migrant students under the supervision of a certificated master teacher. Each tutor is required to write one or more SMART goals that are designed to target and drive their instruction. In 2011–2012, the CMC served an average of 6,000 K-12 migrant students during each fall and spring semesters.

CMC GOAL #1: DIRECT INSTRUCTIONAL SERVICES TO SUPPORT MIGRANT STUDENT ACADEMIC ACHIEVEMENT

CMC Summer Program

During the summer the CMC employs over 375 tutors who are enrolled not only in the CMC college sites, but accepts applications from candidates enrolled in any California community college, four year university-state or private independent IHE. They are placed in migrant impacted summer schools throughout the state, some living in the migrant labor camps along with the migrant families. As in the regular year, these tutors work under the supervision of certified summer school teachers. CMC students are employed from 8 to 14 weeks during the summer, providing instructional services to nearly 7,000 migrant students during the summer.

The CMC summer component also incorporates Outdoor Education (OE) and Puppetry programs. The OE program targets fourth through sixth grade migrant students that have not had the opportunity to experience an OE summer camp during the regular school year due to their migrant mobility. The program operates for a period of seven to eight weeks with two OE teams each serving approximately 100 students at various outdoor education camps throughout the state per week. In its early years more than 5,000 migrant students participated in an outdoor education summer camp experience. The programs were directed by former CMC students who after years of teaching had continued their education and earned an administrative or counseling credential. The OE program strives to: (a) instill a respect and appreciation for nature; (b) develop self-confidence and leadership skills; and (c) increase a student's knowledge base around select science and environmental education concepts.

The CMC recruits and trains 25 to 30 of its advanced school year tutors to participate in the summer Puppetry Program. In the Puppetry program, CMC tutors learn the art of puppetry making, writing scripts, and performing puppetry presentations. Once trained, these puppeteers work in teams of two and perform puppetry presentations to migrant students in schools throughout the state. The presentations focus on health, social and safety issues such as water and fire safety, anti-bullying, developing self-confidence and dental hygiene. Puppeteer tutors learn important teaching skills (e.g., public speaking, use of realia) that will help them become effective teachers. During the summer of 2012, these puppeteers presented to nearly 5,000 migrant students throughout the state. Another component that was in existence in CMC's early years was the CMC Medi-Corps program. This program recruited former migrant students who were interested in the health profession. Their role was similar to the Puppetry program where teams of two Medi-Corps participants were assigned to the summer school program to provide lessons on health education and nutrition that address challenges affecting migrant students and their families. Just as many CMC alumni have become teachers, principals, superintendents, counselors, and professors in universities (such as these two authors have), many Medi-Corps alumni have become health educators, nurses and physicians.

CMC GOAL # 2: DEVELOPING A CADRE OF FUTURE BILINGUAL-BICULTURAL TEACHERS

CMC's second goal is to develop a cadre of future credentialed bilingual educators who will be better equipped to work with migrant students. Besides program data that is collected yearly, there has been doctoral dissertations and academic journals written on the CMC program effectiveness, but at a minimal level. CMC testimonials are an important factor to consider in its success. A doctoral dissertation study conducted by Gonzalez (2012) affirms the positive impact that the CMC has had on the preparation and credentialing of migrant workers in the field of education. In his study, he surveyed 105 CMC alumni, of which 96% were currently in an education occupation (e.g., teacher, administrator, college professor, or related position). The survey specifically explored the impact of participation in Mini-Corps on completion of an undergraduate degree, completion of a credentialing program, obtaining employment, professional development, and establishing a mentor/mentee relationship. Gonzalez's data establishes a positive correlation to obtaining an undergraduate degree and his findings make a strong case for the impact on completion of the credentialing program at their respective institutions. He supports his assertions with data collected from interviews with five CMC respondents. In response to the survey question, do you feel that participation in the Mini-Corps Program influenced your decision to pursue a teaching credential, one alumni stated,

> Because of Mini-Corps, I got to know some of the staff. The professors were going to be the [same] ones for the teaching credentials. I felt more comfortable applying to that credentialing program than I did applying to the others, so in a way it would kind of seem like I was moving along. It didn't seem like a big transition from graduating to getting into a credential program. The work was a lot in the program but I felt that I had been trained already. (Gonzalez, p. 111)

Gonzalez's data also demonstrated that respondents' participation in CMC positively impacted their employment opportunities. Gonzalez (2012) writes:

> All of the alumni offered a positive response and believed that they obtained employment by either establishing a networking system or by feeling prepared for the interview process because of their experiences within Mini-Corps. The alumni thought that Mini-Corps provided a networking system that assisted in obtaining a job. An interviewee stated, "If it wasn't for Mini-Corps, I wouldn't have had this big of a chance over other people who wanted, to work in the same district." Some alumni believed that the knowledge they learned regarding teaching strategies assisted them during the interview process, and as a result they obtained employment. An alum declared, "Without a doubt, I felt prepared; I wasn't nervous. I felt good; I knew what I was going to do because of the Mini-Corps experience. (pp. 147)

Based on his findings Gonzalez (2012) makes this observation about the overall preparation alumni receive before entering the teaching workforce,

> The undergraduate experience provides the foundation for Mini-Corps tutors to develop as teachers prior to graduating. When the tutors reach the credential program, there is an ethos of possessing a repertoire of practices with regard to teaching-related professional behaviors that assist them in completing a credentialing program and obtaining employment. (p. 131)

Mini-Corps tutors become well versed in tackling the challenges that arise when working with an ethnically and linguistically diverse student population. The CMC tutors understand the challenges migrant students and their families face on a daily basis. Therefore, they are both academically and instructionally prepared for entering a teaching credentialing program. A high sense of self-efficacy results in having more confidence when teaching. For the most part, tutors may be more knowledgeable regarding relational interactions with migrant students and their families than other credentialed candidates who have not had similar experiences. For example, Gonzalez (2012) noted alumni interviewed discussed the importance of learning how to plan, construct and write a lesson plan even before entering their credentialing program. Also, alumni noted that "Mini-Corps assisted in developing a professional binder, and how to write a cover letter and resume when seeking employment. Mini-Corps even assisted in filling out applications for teaching positions" (p. 131).

It is evident that the Mini-Corps program also enhanced alumni's instructional strategies associated with working with migrants. For instance, the fourth question in Gonzales's interview is, what specific skills did participation in the Mini-Corps Program foster or help you develop? How have these skills impacted your career? He explains, "The responses indicated skills pertaining to understanding the struggles of migrants, interacting with parents, constructing a professional binder, best practices in working with students in the classroom, and reflecting on the tutors' instructional practices were routinely practiced...

they became more of a parent advocate, and their skills pertaining to working with parents were honed in because of their involvement with Mini-Corps" (pp. 131–132).

PROGRAM DATA COLLECTION TO SUPPORT PROGRAM IMPACT

In 2011, the program embarked on a journey to examine and collect data on program impact. This was made possible since the central office stored files for a large number of former Mini-Corps tutor participants. A simple Excel database was developed that captured the following data: Tutor Name, Social Security Number, Date of Birth, Gender, Last Program Site, Start and End Dates, Major, Type of Credential and Date Received. The data entry for former tutor participants was completed in December 2011. Central office staff proceeded to cross-reference data for each former tutor against the Commission on Teaching Credentialing (CTC) database to secure information on whether a credential was earned, the type of credential and when it was received. The data confirmed what we surmised intuitively and through anecdotal data, but provided hard numbers that speaks to the effectiveness of the program and its success in meeting the second major program goal over the last thirty years.

As Figure 3.3 indicates (see below), nearly 60% of the tutors in this data subset received one or more credentials. At the time that this report was prepared comparison data for similar programs was not readily available. When this information was shared with program coordinators they anticipated that the percentage receiving credentials would be higher, more like 70%. However, the data was not disaggregated by year to determine if some differences were related to time period, or changes in program structure. This will be done in the future in order to maintain more appropriate records.

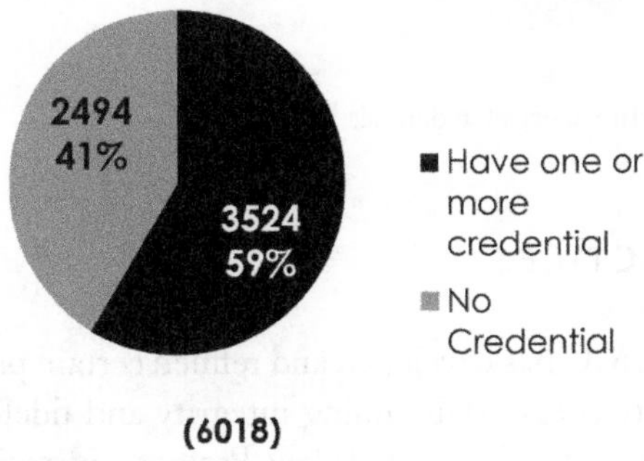

Figure 3.3. Number of California Mini-Corps Former Tutors Receiving One or More Credentials.

Figure 3.4 below identifies the types of credentials received based on the information available. Of the 3,524 former tutors in this data set, over 2,100 received multiple subject credentials and 565 received single subject credentials. It is interesting to note that another 1,856 received Bilingual/Cross-cultural credentials and 350 received ELD/ESL credentials. This data point is important because a goal of the program is to produce future teachers who are more sensitive and equipped to address the academic needs of English learners and migrant students. The fact that over 70% of these former teachers earned a bilingual/cross cultural, ELD/ESL, or multiple subject credential, speaks to the additional training and schooling that these former participants received to enable them to provide appropriate instructional programs for migrant and English learner students. The shades on the pie chart in Figure 3.4 reports the types of credentials earned—Single Subject, Multiple Subject, ELD/ESL, Bilingual/Cross Cultural, Administrative Services, Other, and Unknown credentials.

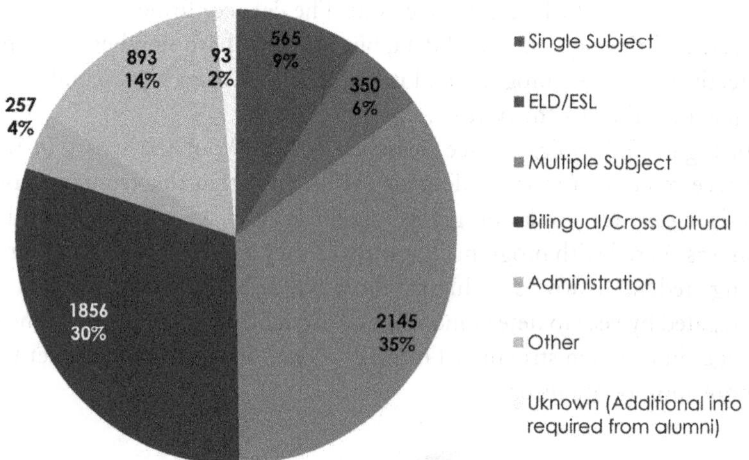

Figure 3.4. California Mini-Corps Credentials Received.

CMC BEST PRACTICES

Over the years the CMC has developed and refined certain practices and strategies to improve its effectiveness. Maintaining integrity and fidelity in the implementation of program at each college site is key. Program administrators monitor and evaluate each program year through on-site visits, meetings with college/university liaisons and Migrant Education staff, and observations of coordinators and tutors at the school site. Tutor applicants undergo a stringent two-phase selection process that includes a face-to-face interview by the local program coordinator and an application packet review by central office administration.

CMC invests and understands the role of comprehensive professional development in producing desired results. The program uses a trainer of trainer model for professional development. Each year program coordinators participate in at least six days of training by current and expert researchers. The training content focuses on effective teaching strategies in English language arts (ELA), English language development (ELD) and mathematics; developing professional learning communities (PLC); implementation of common core standards; cognitive coaching; and other relevant subjects. Collaboration time is built into each training session to brainstorm and discuss application strategies. In turn, each coordinator is required to provide six hours of professional development each month for their tutors. Training modules for tutors include lesson design, classroom management, English Language Arts, English Language Leaners, mathematics and assessment. The tutors are expected to apply and practice strategies learned in their on-going tutoring sessions. Time is built into monthly meetings to debrief their practice in Professional Learning Community teams.

Early on, CMC recognized the power of reflective teaching to improve a teacher's craft and professional development. To support its professional development for both coordinators and tutors, CMC integrates an intensive Cognitive Coaching (CC) model into its program. Coordinators participate in an eight day CC training and receive refreshers on ongoing basis. Coordinators are expected to conduct at least two informal observations for each tutor each month. After observing the tutor in action, the coordinator debriefs with the tutor using CC mediation questions intended to guide the tutor through a self-reflection process. Tutors learn to critically examine their practice with the goal improving their instruction and expanding their teaching repertoire. During the site visits, coordinators also orient supervising teachers regarding their roles and interact with them and principals to assess tutor performance, discuss placements, and other relevant topics.

Finally, tutors receive a wealth of practice. For tutors who begin their CMC experience as college freshmen, they accumulate more than 2,000 hours of direct tutoring in individual or small group settings with multiple grade levels. This practicum prepares and places them much further ahead than their non-CMC student teaching counterparts. Each year, coordinators alter tutors' placements. This practice not only helps tutors find their "teaching niche" but it also exposes them to a variety of teaching styles. It is not uncommon for student teacher supervisors to comment on how advanced and prepared CMC tutors are for their teaching assignments once they have been admitted into a teacher education program.

LOOKING AT CMC RESULTS

Each year CMC summarizes its annual accomplishments in a year-end report that describes the program, its goals, services provided as well as student and tutor outcomes. During the 2010–2012 program years, under the state CMC program director and one of the co-authors of this chapter, Dr. Ernesto Ruiz, CMC conducted an evaluation pilot study to more accurately determine the level of tutoring impact on migrant student academic progress. As a result of this evaluation pilot study, existing teacher surveys were refined to ensure more validity and reliability. Table 3.2 summarizes the findings for the teacher surveys conducted in 2011–2012.

Table 3.2. California Mini-Corps (CMC) Tutoring Impact 2011–2012.

	Tutoring Impact (All School Levels)							
	None (%)	Minimal (%)	Some (%)	Significant (%)	Unsure (%)	N/A (%)	Total	
Mathematics	0.98	4.68	27.97	49.84	4.13	12.4	100%	919
English Language Arts	0.45	4.92	31.54	52.24	5.37	5.48	100%	894

CMC Master Teachers for both content areas completed an average of 907 surveys. Nearly 50% and 52%, respectively, responded that Mini-Corps tutoring had "Significant" impact on their migrant students' academic progress in Mathematics and English Language Arts respectively. Another 28% and 32% of teachers surveyed responded that Mini-Corps tutoring had "Some" impact on their migrant students' academic progress in Mathematics and English Language Arts, respectively. These results are significant considering the number of respondents and the percentage of CMC Master Teachers that responded affirmatively to this question; nearly 80% in Mathematics and over 80% in English Language Arts.

In addition to assessing perceived tutoring impact on ELA and mathematics, surveys were also conducted to assess perceived tutor impact on ten non-academic student engagement indicators. Table 3.3 reports the results of the ten non-academic Student Engagement Indicators. The results for the teacher surveys related to impact on these student engagement indicators positively affirmed the important role that Mini-Corps tutors play in helping migrant students with school/classroom activities and responsibilities that influence academic success. Over 1,035 surveys were completed, and an average of 47% of CMC Master Teachers perceived that Mini-Corps tutors had "Significant" impact on these migrant student behaviors. When the average percentages for these two responses, "Significant" and "Some" are combined, over 70% of CMC Master Teachers responded affirmatively to this question. The data indicates that those behaviors exhibited in class (e.g. following teacher directions, following classroom rules, completing classroom assignments) received the highest rankings in terms of impact on students. This makes sense, since the teacher directly observes and is better able to assess the work and interactions between tutor and migrant students in her/his classroom.

Table 3.3. California Mini-Corps (CMC) Student Engagement Indicators 2011–2012.

Student Engagement Indicators (All School Levels)								
	None (%)	A Little (%)	Some (%)	Significant (%)	Unsure (%)	N/A (%)	Total	
Following teacher directions	2.02	7.02	32.98	52.21	5.77	0	100%	1040
Following classroom rules	4.14	6.45	32.44	48.99	7.99	0	100%	1039
Completing class assignments	3.07	6.14	34.23	51.49	5.08	0	100%	1043
Turning in fully completed homework	9.41	5.86	27.38	39.48	17.87	0	100%	1041
Turning in homework on time	11.36	6.64	25.31	36.96	19.73	0	100%	1039
Listening attentively to the teacher	3.75	9.04	31.44	47.12	8.65	0	100%	1040
Participating in whole class discussions	5.1	9.91	31.28	44.95	8.76	0	100%	1039
Working effectively in peer groups	2.98	7.99	30.32	49.86	8.85	0	100%	1039
Attending class regularly	10.59	5.49	17.32	34.55	32.05	0	100%	1039
Getting to school on time	11.68	5.31	15.83	32.92	34.27	0	100%	1036

REPLICATING THE CMC PROGRAM MODEL

There are several important considerations for states or agencies interested in replicating the CMC program model. Since the project sites recruit college students, developing or identifying and existing partnership with an Institute of Higher Education (IHE) is critical. A formal presentation to key university stakeholders on the model, purpose and rationale, and its benefits to the university and school districts will go a long way in selling the program concept. Once the site has been identified, having a university contact will expedite operational arrangements on campus (e.g., office space, classroom space for workshops, telephone and internet service). This contact person will also become an advocate for the program and can facilitate the processing of the memoranda of understanding through university channels.

In determining the selection of a university site, it is also important to consider the pool of potential tutor candidates, especially if the project is going to serve a specialized student population such as migrant students. If tutor eligibility includes specific criteria (e.g., migrant background, bilingual, low income), assessing potential numbers and communication with admissions office is obviously a first step. Collaboration with other university programs (i.e., CAMP, EOPS, TRIO and summer bridge programs) is critical and highly recommended. Many CMC project site offices are located in the student services building that house these programs. This proximity facilitates referrals, collaboration and mutual support.

As discussed previously, a comprehensive professional development component is essential to the success of the program. Educational research is clear about the critical role that high quality professional development plays for those delivering instruction and for raising student academic achievement. The trainer of trainer model has served CMC well. This model is both cost efficient and reaches over 400 tutors each year. Additionally, the transference of new knowledge and teaching skills gained from the workshop setting to the school site increases through the monthly site visits conducted by the program coordinators. Program coordinators use the cognitive coaching process to reinforce skills and strategies presented in monthly workshops and to help students reflect on their practice.

Ongoing communication with the site principals and supervising teachers cannot be over emphasized, especially when assessing tutor placement and performance. Establishing positive working relationships with both parties will facilitate other tasks such as completing surveys and assisting with tutor's SMART goal. If the principal and teacher view the tutors as positive contributors to their schools, they become the program's strongest advocates and invite future tutors with open arms.

Through a cadre of well-trained college tutors, the program has served many thousands of migrant students throughout the state of California since its inception. These services have helped migrant students improve academically and graduate from high school. Just as important, is the systemic impact CMC has had on California's public school system. CMC has helped improve the teaching landscape by producing thousands of bilingual/bicultural teachers over the last four decades. These teachers have and continue to positively impact the lives of thousands of migrant and EL students annually. Additionally, many of these teachers are now in leadership positions as principals, administrators, superintendents, university administrators and professors. They teach and lead with a certain culturally proficient passion and commitment that distinguishes them. They continue to advocate and improve public education for California's students who have the highest educational needs.

DISCUSSION AND IMPLICATIONS

There are many exemplary and innovative preservice teacher programs in the United States and globally, but in order to be at the cutting edge, Schools of Education and teacher preparation programs must continue planning and implementing innovative preservice teacher preparation programs. If colleges of education fail to do so it may result in continuing to perpetuate traditional and stagnant teacher preparation programs that do not meet the emerging needs of our teacher candidates as well as serve the ethnically diverse student populations in our schools, in this case, our migrant students who continue to be one of the most underserved student populations.

Quezada, Kinsey and Louque (2016) discuss the need to develop and create innovative preparation programs in California and nationally, and pose the following points of consideration that are also relevant to reform teacher preparation.

1. *Change is never easy*: Models of teacher preparation licensure programs cannot remain stagnant. They must transition from the "traditional coursework model" of teacher certification to more "alternative internship models."
2. *Implementing 21st century skills goes beyond the classroom*: Professional teacher preparation standards such as the Teacher Performance Expectations that were just recently passed by the California Commission on Teacher Credentialing in June 2016 need to be followed as guides. Today's educational climate requires teachers who can negotiate the 21st century skills needed to meet the educational needs of 21st century students. The 21st century skills movement has been praised for its goal setting and its call for learning to think and work collaboratively and creatively. However,

one criticism is the lack of specific guidance for schools, teachers, and school leaders. This means that teacher preparation programs need to be developing "teacher leaders" who are capable of taking the latest research on teaching and learning and evidence-based data to serve the complex educational challenges faced by teachers and students.

3. *Professional Standards*: Establishing best teaching practices for creating high-achieving schools in the form of standards is a challenge that we will continue to face. These teaching practices have evolved into standards for teacher preparation programs such as the Council of Accreditation for Educator Preparation Programs (CAEP), the California Standards for the Teaching Performance (CSTP), and the California Teaching Performance Expectations (TPE) standards. These standards set the bar for both traditional and alternative teacher preparation licensure and certification programs so they may parallel equivalent skills needed of all future teachers, and teacher leaders.
4. *Creating Alternative Pathways*: New and innovative pathways for teaching positions can be addressed through alternative licensure, certification, accreditation changes, and more experiential clinical practice. The one-size fits all teacher preparation and outreach models are archaic and do not meet the new technological advances in program delivery in and out of the classroom. New instructional modalities and strategies such as on-line delivery, MOOCS, utilization of TedTalks, iPads/Tablets, interactive television/distance education, as well as others, need to be implemented. Of most importance is diversifying the ethnic pool of future teachers, and administrators; therefore, implementing alternative recruitment efforts to increase the candidate teacher pipeline is a must. As the portrait of the California Mini-Corps program illustrates, tailoring teaching and learning experiences for young adults must start in the early years, in middle school, high school and particularly at the community college level, in order to provide a continuum of professional development. For low income students a paid clinical experience such as the one provided by the California Mini-Corps program through the Butte County Office of Education throughout California assures college students that they will have part-time employment for their four to five years of college as well as in the summer. These learning experiences across the span of their college years are vital for developing a pipeline of effective future teachers. Forming partnerships between K-12 school districts and institutions of higher education to provide support and networking for future teachers is also as important.

5. *Teacher Preparation Innovation*: School of Education teacher preparation programs train future teachers to prepare them for a myriad of teaching situations. Candidates in teacher preparation programs must practice the latest teaching methods and practices for culturally and linguistically diverse teaching for the students and school community they will teach and lead in the future. Developing these skills in teachers will help to increase their ability and knowledge regarding how to collaborate and communicate effectively with other teachers, staff, parents, and community members (Louque & Latunde, 2014).

SUMMARY

We know from the research that the classroom teacher is the most important person to have an impact on student achievement. Therefore, various Schools of Education, in partnership with county offices of education and school districts, have worked to better prepare teachers through nontraditional alternative teacher preparation models so they may further support the pipeline of new teachers to create a diverse teaching force in our nations schools. This effort can help to raise the academic achievement of students and close the ethnic teacher representation gap. To our knowledge, the California Mini-Corps Program, funded by California Migrant Education Program as part of the federal Department of Education-Migrant Education Division in partnership with the Butte County Office of Education, is the only program in the nation that has been in existence for 50 years that has resulted in an increase in the recruitment of future bilingual-bicultural teachers who come from migrant farmworker backgrounds to teach migrant farmworker children. This program has produced thousands of bilingual teachers, administrators, counselors and professors, yet it has never been replicated in other states, either by other Migrant Education Programs or other teacher recruitment pipeline type programs. Therefore, the California Mini-Corps Program is the "best kept secret" in California as an alternative early clinical experience model of teacher preparation to meet the needs of our culturally and linguistically diverse student population.

REFERENCES

Butte County Office of Education. (2012). *2010–2011 Annual evaluation report: California Mini Corps*. Retrieved April 15, 2016 from www.bcoe.org

California Department of Education. (2016). *California public school enrollment district report*. Retrieved April 1, 2016 from CDE Website: http://data1.cde.ca.gov/dataquest/

Darling-Hammond, L., Furger, R., Shields, M. P., & Sutcher, L. (2016). *Addressing California's teacher shortage: An analysis of sources and solutions*. Palo Alto, CA: Learning Policy Institute.

Gonzalez, E. (2012). *The impact of participation in the Mini-Corps program as an undergraduate on alumni's professional career*. Doctoral Dissertation. Sacramento, CA: Sacramento State University.

Interstate Migrant Education Council (1988). *Annual report 1987–1988: A special project of the education commission of the states*. Retrieved from: http://files.eric.ed.gov/fulltext/ED305206.pdf

KPBS Public Broadcasting. (2015). *California ranks as world's 8th largest economy, overtaking Russia and Italy*. Retrieved August 25, 2015 from http://www.kpbs.org/news/2014/jul/08/california-ranks-worlds-8th-largest-economy-overta/

Lindsey, R., Robins, K., & Terrell, D. (2009). *Cultural proficiency: A manual for school leaders*. Thousand Oaks, CA: Corwin Press.

Louque, A., & Latunde, Y. (2014). Supporting preservice teachers' collaboration with school leaders. *The Journal of School Public Relations, 35*(4), 494–510.

Quezada, L. R., Kinsey, G., & Louque, C. A. (2016). Preparing quality school administrator licensure programs in North America: Innovation in the state of California. In A. M. Flores & T. Barwani (Eds.), *Redefining teacher education for the post-2015 global era: Global challenges and best practices*. Hauppauge, NY: Nova Publishers

Quezada, L. R., Lindsey, R., & Lindsey, D. (2012). *Culturally proficient practice supporting educators of English learning students*. Thousand Oaks, CA: Corwin Press.

Quezada, L. R., & Louque, C. A. (2004). The absence of diversity in the academy: Faculty of color in educational administration programs. *Education, 125*(2), 213–221.

Quezada, L. R., Rodríguez-Valls, F., & Lindsey, R. (2016). *Teaching and supporting migrant children in our schools: A culturally proficient approach*. Lanham, MD: Rowman & Littlefield Publishing Group.

U.S. Census Bureau (2016). *Quick facts, California*. Retrieved from: https://www.census.gov/quickfacts/fact/table/CA#viewtop

U.S. Department of Education (2016). *Migrant education program*. Retrieved from: https://www2.ed.gov/programs/mep/guidance/prelim_pg3.html

California Mini-Corps Commentary

BELINDA BUSTOS FLORES

As social-justice oriented educators and researchers, we often speak about the need for equitable education that counters neoliberal structures that are fraught with racism and oppression. While it is important to recognize the numerous societal oppressive factors, such as educational opportunity gaps, income inequalities, employment opportunities, I will reserve my commentary to the early recruitment of potential bilingual candidates as a conduit for equitable representation among the teacher corps as this is the foci of the California Mini-Corps Migrant Teacher Assistant Program.

Foremost, the critical shortage of bilingual educators cannot be underscored (U.S. Department of Education, 2015) when considering the demographic trends present in such states as California and Texas, in which Latinos are the majority population. Nationally, this demographic shift is ever so evident among the young (age < 5) Latino U.S. population, who are projected to be the emerging majority school population in the next five years (Fry & Passel, 2009; Santiago, Galdeano, & Taylor, 2015).

These Latino children are also likely to be bilingual learners, with Spanish as their first language. Hence, in the case of bilingual and second language learners, to ensure equitable education, we must also strive for a teaching force with a linguistic competency (Guerrero, 2003; Lucas, Villegas, & Freedson-Gonzalez, 2008) and bilingual capacity to deliver content (Aquino-Sterling, 2016; Guerrero & Valadez, 2011). Given the needs of a growing population of bilingual learners, we can no longer be complacent in ensuring equitable representation through the active recruitment of bilingual educators.

In recruiting bilingual educators, several strategies have shown to be successful, such as growing your own or career ladder (Flores, Keehn, & Perez, 2002; Valenciana, Weisman, & Flores, 2006; Valenzuela, 2015), creating college-university partnerships (Flores & Claeys, 2010/2011; Valenciana, Morin, & Morales, 2005), online programs for rural communities (Lohfink, Morales, Shroyer, Yahnke, & Hernandez, 2011) and retooling foreign-trained teachers (*normalistas*) as bilingual educators (Flores & Clark, 2002; Salazar, 2003). The California Mini-Corps Teacher Assistant Program is a prime example of a successful systemic effort in the early recruitment of teachers and credentialing of bilingual educators.

I am in agreement with Quezada's and Ruiz's premise, that an equitable representation among the teacher corps will counter educational gaps, which could ultimately increase employment opportunities, and thereby, reduce income inequalities. To ensure equitable representation requires that there is a pipeline in which specific groups are targeted. Quezada and Ruiz clearly justify the inherent value of recruiting potential bilingual teachers who can serve as role models, specifically those whose lives mirror those of their students.

As a systemic effort, unique to California's Mini-Corps is the recruitment of young migrant high school students. In targeting a specific subpopulation, such as migrant students, the Mini-Corps is attempting to ensure cultural synchronicity (Villegas & Irvine, 2010). Not all Latinos or bilingual educators have had the experience of working in the fields. While teachers can be empathetic to the plight of migrant students, Latino teachers, who were migrants, know their students' experiences first hand, and are likely confident in using these experiences to anchor teaching and provide enriching opportunities to learn.

The value of cultural synchronicity (Villegas & Irvine, 2010) cannot be ignored as a growing body of research supports this contention (Flores, Sheets, & Clark, 2011; Sleeter, Neal, & Kumashiro, 2015; Sleeter & Thao, 2007; Tandon, Bianco, & Zion, 2015; Villegas, Strom, & Lucas, 2012). This premise is further anchored in studies that have demonstrated that equitable representation addresses the educational gap that often occurs in high ethnic and racial minority schools. That is, cultural and/or racial synchronicity academically benefits students of color as well as their white counterparts (Dee, 2004; Eddy & Easton-Brooks, 2011; Egalite, Kisida, & Winters, 2015; Meier, Wrinkle, & Polinard, 1999).

While ethnic/racial representation is indeed a step towards a positive direction, as is demonstrated in the Mini-Corps, we must also consider the heterogeneity present in bilingual education classrooms. There are bilingual learners who are recent arrivals as well as others who are first generation immigrants and beyond. These nuances further highlight the importance of recruiting bilinguals with similar cultural and linguistic experiences. We cannot assume that all Latinos are bilingual or that bilinguals have the bilingual proficiency needed to deliver academic content and assist learners in developing their bilingualism. Further, we cannot simply discount individuals if they do not fully demonstrate proficiency in both languages. It is important to consider that the U. S. schooling experiences for bilinguals has been one of eradication of the native language rather than the promotion of bilingualism (Guerrero & Valadez, 2011; Sutterby, Ayala, & Murillo, 2005). Hence, language learning opportunities must be part of the bilingual education teacher preparation program (Guerrero & Valadez, 2011). While not specifically discussed by Quezada and Ruiz in this chapter, the field and service leaning experiences built into the project hopefully provides Mini-Corps participants with opportunities to acquire the academic language needed to be proficient in both languages. Moreover, these apprenticeship experiences should also serve to equip Mini-Corps participants with critical bilingual/bicultural pedagogy and develop critical consciousness (Flores, Hernández, García, & Claeys, 2011).

As previously stated, the recruitment of potential bilingual teachers also requires a concerted effort from the teacher preparation program in which there is attention to the needs of recruits. For example, *Project Alianza* was a binational effort between the U.S. and the Mexico in which the goal was to increase the number of bilingual educators from targeted groups (Flores & Clark, 2002). Several universities across Texas and California tapped into the cultural and human capital of the community by recruiting and preparing resident *normalistas* (foreign-trained teachers) and paraprofessionals to become credentialed bilingual educators. Each group had specific assets, such as degree of bilingualism and biliteracy as well as pedagogical knowledge and skills. In the case of the majority of *normalistas*, it was evident that they had a strong command of academic Spanish, yet their English proficiency was at a conversational level. *Normalistas* also held deep understanding of the Mexican schooling system and pedagogical skills for teaching literacy. Conversely, the paraprofessionals' academic English was stronger than their Spanish; moreover, they had extensive understanding of the U.S. schooling system and bilingual/bicultural pedagogy. In addition to having a cohort model and a variety of field experiences, coursework was offered in English and Spanish. The cohort model served as learning community providing both groups opportunities to demonstrate their strengths, address their biliteracy development, and confront pervasive attitudes each group held about the other group (Flores & Clark, 2002). As a result of these efforts, both groups, but especially *normalistas*, who had been an untapped capital residing within our communities, were now seen as having the potential to serve as U. S. bilingual educators. As a systemic effort, *Project Alianza* also addressed admission barriers such as English proficiency requirements and the credentialing of foreign transcripts. Upon completion of their program of study, school districts highly sought and hired the *Alianzistas* because of their capabilities to meet the needs and ensure the success of their bilingual student population.

As role models, bilingual educators are not only a reflection of the students in the classroom, but also can bolster the academic achievement of their students. As such, Quezada and Ruiz provided evidence that the tutoring has indeed supported the migrant tutee's mathematic and reading academic progress as well as other types of positive student behavior. Similarly, in the case of *Project Alianza*, the resident *normalistas'* knowledge and skills as Mexican teachers was invaluable especially in working with recent arrivals. Likewise, the paraprofessionals had deep knowledge of the community that they readily used to connect with the students (Flores, Keehn, & Pérez, 2002; Pérez, Flores, & Strecker, 2003). Indeed, these bilingual educators, as contended Villegas, Strom, and Lucas (2012), are "uniquely positioned to teach" (p. 287) their respective students.

Nevertheless, in ensuring that bilingual educators remain culturally efficacious in their practices, as realized by Quezada and Ruiz, they must also be prepared to assist their students with developing transportable 21st century skills. Greater attention to the use of digital skills and the acquisition of multiliteracies is paramount during the teacher preparation program. Moreover, greater focus on the acquisition of critical bilingual/bicultural knowledge and practices are needed. Apprenticeships with master bilingual education teachers can support the Mini-Corps participants' development and commitment to teaching in bilingual settings.

Quezada and Ruiz concluded that the California Mini-Corps Teacher Assistant Program has also been successful in recruiting, preparing, and credentialing Latino teachers. As Ingersoll, Merrill, and Stuckey (2014) recently observed, trends demonstrate an increase of ethnic/racial representation in the teaching force and suggested that minority recruitment efforts have been successful in increasing the number of ethnic/racial minority teachers. Nevertheless, despite these efforts, there is still an overwhelming representation of White teachers. Further, along with recruitment and preparation of bilingual educators, we must consider their retention as a means to ensure equitable representation (Villegas et al., 2012).

While Quezada and Ruiz do not provide us specific information on teacher employment placement and retention, they do reveal that some of their Mini-Corps participants are now in leadership positions and are advocates for the migrant population. Similar trends are noted for *Project Alianza*, with *Alianzistas* becoming career bilingual educators and leaders within their school districts. Indeed the literature reveals that in terms of teacher representation and retention in high-need schools, Teachers of Color are more likely to be present and remain in the field than their counterparts (Ingersoll, Merrill, & Stuckey, 2014). At the same time, they are also more likely to teach in hard-to-staff urban communities (Ingersoll & Merrill, 2017). Given that bilingual educators, as other Teachers of

Color, are often driven to pursue teaching as a means to ensure social justice, this may explain their retention in high need schools (Claeys, 2011; Flores, Ek, & Sánchez, 2011). As Quezada and Ruiz also revealed, their Mini-Corps participants maintain their passion and commitment to teaching, but there is a need for more qualitative data to better understand the experiences of these former migrants turned teachers given they often face the demands of hard to staff schools (Ingersoll & May, 2011; Ingersoll et al., 2014).

Overall, the California Mini-Corps Migrant Teacher Assistant Program is an innovative program should be commended for its sustained efforts over the years. Other states facing bilingual educator shortages should strive to develop pipelines from their emerging Latino populations. To meet immediate needs, the recruitment of potential bilingual teachers requires a multipronged approach and multiple entry points. This includes growing your own from existing paraprofessional staff or from second-career individuals. I also recommend that these same states canvas their recent immigrants and identify those who have foreign teacher credentials or other degreed individuals who can get credentialed as bilingual educators. Finally, since we have learned more about the type of preparation required for bilingual educators to be culturally efficacious and who are retained as career teachers (Flores, Sheets, & Clark, 2011), we need to ensure recruitment is coupled with rigorous preparation and continual opportunities for learning and development.

REFERENCES

Aquino-Sterling, C. R. (2016). Responding to the call: Developing and assessing pedagogical Spanish competencies in bilingual teacher education. *Bilingual Research Journal, 39*(1), 50–68. doi: 10.1080/15235882.2016.1139519

Claeys, L. (2011). *Teacher motivation to teach and to remain teaching culturally and linguistically diverse students.* The University of Texas at San Antonio, 2011, 208; 3454071

Dee, T. (2004). Teachers, race, and student achievement in a randomized experiment. *The Review of Economics and Statistics, 86*(1), 195–210.

Eddy, C. M., & Easton-Brooks, D. (2011). Ethnic matching, school placement, and mathematic achievement of African American students from kindergarten through fifth grade. *Urban Education, 46*(6), 1280–1299. doi: 10.1177/0042085911413149

Egalite, A. J., Kisida, B., & Winters, M. A. (2015). Representation in the classroom: The effect of own race teachers on student achievement. *Economics of Education Review, 45*, 44–52. doi: 10.1016j

Flores, B. B., & Claeys, L. (2010/2011). Academy for Teacher Excellence: Maximizing synergy among partners for promoting college access for Latino teacher candidates. *The Urban Review, 43*(3), 321–338. doi:10.1007/s11256-010-0153

Flores, B. B., & Clark, E. R. (2002). *El desarrollo de Proyecto Alianza: Lessons learned and policy implications.* CBER, Arizona State University.

Flores, B. B., Ek, L., & Sánchez, P. (2011). Bilingual education candidate ideology: Descubriendo sus motives y creencias. In B. B. Flores, R. H. Sheets, & E. R. Clark (Eds.), *Teacher preparation for bilingual student populations: Educar para transformar* (pp. 40–58). New York: Routledge.

Flores, B. B., Hernández, A., García, C. T., & Claeys, L. (2011). Teacher Academy Learning Community's induction support: Guiding teachers through their zone of professional development. *Journal of Mentoring and Tutoring: Partnership in Learning, 19*(3), 365–389. doi: 10.1080/13611267.2011.597124

Flores, B. B., Keehn, S., & Pérez, B. P. (2002). Critical need for bilingual education teachers: The potentiality of *normalistas* and paraprofessionals. *Bilingual Research Journal, 26*(3), 687–708.

Flores, B. B., Sheets, R. H., & Clark, E. R. (2011). *Teacher preparation for bilingual student populations: Educar para transformar*. New York: Routledge.

Fry, R., & Passel, J. E. (2009). *Latino children: A majority are U.S. born offspring of immigrants*. Washington, DC: Pew Hispanic Center. Retrieved June 15, 2014 from http://www.pewhispanic.org/2009/05/28/latino-children-a-majority-are-us-born-offspring-of-immigrants/

Guerrero, M. D. (2003). Acquiring and participating in the use of academic Spanish: Four novice Latina bilingual education teachers' stories. *Journal of Latinos and Education, 2*(3), 159–181.

Guerrero, M. D., & Valadez, C. (2011). Fostering candidate Spanish language development. In B. B. Flores, R. H. Sheets, & E. R. Clark (Eds.), *Teacher preparation for bilingual student populations: Educar para transformar* (pp. 59–72). New York, NY: Routledge.

Ingersoll, R. M., & May, H. (2011). *Recruitment, retention and the minority teacher shortage. Consortium for policy research in education*. CPRE Research Report #RR-69. Retrieved from http://repository.upenn.edu/cgi/viewcontent.cgi?article=1232&context=gse_pubs

Ingersoll, R. M., & Merrill, L. (2017). *A Quarter Century of Changes in the Elementary and Secondary Teaching Force: From 1987 to 2012*. Statistical Analysis Report (NCES 2017-092). U.S. Department of Education. Washington, DC: National Center for Education Statistics. Retrieved from: http://files.eric.ed.gov/fulltext/ED573526.pdf

Ingersoll, R. M., Merrill, L., & Stuckey, D. (2014). *Seven trends: The transformation of the teaching force, updated April 2014*. CPRE Report (#RR-80). Philadelphia, PA: Consortium for Policy Research in Education, University of Pennsylvania. Retrieved from: http://repository.upenn.edu/cgi/viewcontent.cgi?article=1003&context=cpre_researchreports

Lohfink, G., Morales, A., Shroyer, G., Yahnke, S., & Hernandez, C. (2011). A distance delivered teacher education program for rural culturally and linguistically diverse teacher candidates. *The Rural Educator, 33*(1), 25–36.

Lucas, T., Villegas, A. M., & Freedson-Gonzalez, M. (2008). Linguistically responsive teacher education: Preparing classroom teachers to teach English language learners. *Journal of Teacher Education, 59*(4), 361–373.

Meier, K. J., Wrinkle, R. D., & Polinard, J. L. (1999). Representative bureaucracy and distributional equity: Addressing the hard question. *Journal of Politics, 61*(4), 1025–1039.

Pérez, B. P., Flores, B. B., & Strecker, S. (2003). Biliteracy teacher education in the southwest. In N. H. Hornberger (Ed.), *The continua of biliteracy: An ecological framework for educational policy. Research, and practice in multilingual settings* (pp. 207–231). Clevedon: Multilingual Matters.

Salazar, D. L. (2003). *An inquiry into a model for normalista preparation and transfer program to the Texas bilingual education teacher program* (Unpublished Dissertation). Texas Tech University.

Santiago, D. A., Galdeano, E. C., & Taylor, M. (2015). *The condition of latinos in education: 2015 factbook*. Excelencia in Education. Retrieved from http://www.edexcelencia.org/research/2015-fact book

Sleeter, C. E., Neal, L. I., & Kumashiro, K. K. (Eds.). (2015). *Diversifying the teacher workforce: Preparing and retaining highly effective teachers.* New York, NY: Routledge.

Sleeter, C. E., & Thao, Y. (2007). Diversifying the teaching force. *Teacher Education Quarterly, 34*(4), 3–8.

Sutterby, J. A., Ayala, J., & Murillo, S. (2005). El sendero torcido al español the twisted path to spanish]: The development of bilingual teachers' Spanish-language proficiency. *Bilingual Research Journal, 29*(2), 435–452, 497, 499, 501.

Tandon, M., Bianco, M., & Zion, S. (2015). Pathways2Teaching: Being and becoming a 'Rida.' In Sleeter, C. E., Neal, L. I., & Kumashiro, K. K. (Eds.), *Diversifying the teacher workforce: Preparing and retaining highly effective teachers* (pp. 111–125). New York, NY: Routledge.

U.S. Department of Education Office of Postsecondary Education. (2015). *Teacher shortage areas nationwide listing 1990–1991 through 2015–2016.* Retrieved from https://www2.ed.gov/about/offices/list/ope/pol/tsa.pdf

Valenciana, C., Morin, J. A., & Morales, R. S. (2005). Meeting the challenge: Building university school district partnerships for a successful career ladder program for teachers of English learners. *Action in Teacher Education, 27*(1), 82–91.

Valenciana, C., Weisman, E. M., & Flores, S. Y. (2006). Voices and perspectives of Latina paraeducators: The journey toward teacher certification. *The Urban Review, 38*(2), 81–99.

Valenzuela, A. (Ed.). (2015). *Growing critically conscious teachers: A social justice curriculum for educators of Latina/o youth.* New York, NY: Teachers College Press.

Villegas, A. M., & Irvine, J. J. (2010). Diversifying the teaching force: An examination of major arguments. *Urban Review, 42*, 175–192.

Villegas, A. M., Strom, K., & Lucas, T. (2012). Closing the racial/ethnic gap between students of color and their teachers: An elusive goal. *Equity & Excellence in Education, 45*(2), 283–301.

CHAPTER FOUR

Grow Your Own (GYO) Illinois—Creating Teachers and Community Leaders

KATE VAN WINKLE

Figure 4.1. Grow Your Own Illinois Symbol.
Source: Grow Your Own Illinois

Table 4.1. Grow Your Own (GYO) Illinois Program Overview.

Funding Source and Period	The GYO IL budget for FY 2016 is $227,800, which was acquired through private foundation funds. Previously GYO IL was funded through state budget; in 2015, GYO IL received $1.4 million through state budget allocation.
Mission	GYO is a unique partnership of community organizations and institutions of higher education whose mission is to support low-income parents and community members in becoming licensed, highly effective teachers in neighborhood schools. GYO creates a career pathway for individuals who have a passion for teaching, but do not have the means or opportunity to realize that passion. GYO grew out of the work of community groups working in low-income neighborhoods to improve their neighborhood schools. Recognizing the untapped resources in their communities, GYO was created to provide a pipeline of highly effective, justice and community oriented teachers.
Timing of Preparation and Support	Candidates enter the program at various points in their education. Some enter with prior college credits, others enter having never been in college. Candidates complete a traditional college degree with a major in education. The length of time it takes to graduate varies by candidate. The average length of the program is 4–6 years.
Partnerships	The heart of GYO is its partnerships. To successfully identify, train and retain diverse, community focused teachers requires close collaboration among community organizations, higher education institutions and public school districts.
Teacher Retention Rate	GYO has a three year retention rate of 69%.

INTRODUCTION

2016 marks the 10th anniversary of students first taking class under the umbrella of Grow Your Own Teachers. Since its inception, GYO has trained 118 teachers, the majority of whom (91%) are Teachers of Color and 86% of whom are teaching in a high needs school in their communities. While increasing the diversity of the teaching force in Illinois is a driving principle for GYO, equally important is training teachers focused on, familiar with, and committed to, the community in which their school is situated.

During our ten years in this effort, we have learned as many lessons as we have had successes. Perhaps the biggest lesson is how entrenched the problem is. Unfortunately, we have not yet been able to close up shop; the issues that gave rise to the creation of GYO continue to persist today. At this organizational milestone, a consensus has emerged nationally that there is a dire need for more Teachers of Color, yet there are very few solutions or financial resources to address the problem. As one of the few programs across the country that has been able to develop a recipe for graduating diverse teachers, this should be a time of celebration and of sharing best practices. Instead, we find ourselves fighting for the survival of our program.

Many factors collude to make the recruitment, training and retention of diverse teachers an on-going struggle, and the issues in Illinois are similar to those across the nation. Yet, GYO candidates face a unique set of issues because of all they are balancing in their lives; the majority of our students are low-income adults, who work full or part time and have families for whom they are responsible. But some issues are universal. As public school teachers are under attack and have become the scape goats for failing schools, the appeal of the teaching profession is waning. For those racially diverse students who do enter college with the desire to become teachers, they are faced with college affordability issues, the struggles of succeeding as first generation college students and the significant barrier presented by the passage of exams required for entry into colleges of education across the state. And these are just the hurdles to completing their college degree.

Each road block, examined in isolation, might seem an innocuous and surmountable obstacle to becoming a teacher. But taken in concert—the costs, the lack of cultural knowledge related to navigating higher education, and the required passage of a state mandated test that has no established connection to teacher quality—these issues portray political and educational systems, that at every level, do not value students of color, particularly, low-income students of color. As in all things related to race in the United States, it is not an accident that there are not more Teachers of Color; thus all of our efforts must be mindful of the larger systems of oppression that we are working within and working against. Sadly, at this moment in time, training diverse teachers, who are committed to teaching low-income students of color, and many of whom are themselves low-income, is a radical and disruptive act.

ISSUES THAT GAVE RISE TO GYO

The issues in Chicago Public Schools (CPS) that led to the creation of the Grow Your Own Teacher program are as pernicious today as they were ten years ago. Illinois has long had a gap, one of the largest in the country, between the number of Teachers of Color and the number of students of color (Boser, 2014). And this gap is growing and is most pronounced in the lowest income communities across the state (King, Kan, & Aldeman, 2016). Chicago has historically had more Teachers of Color than the rest of the state, but it also has higher percentages of students of color. Yet, even in Chicago, the trends are disheartening. In the last 15 years the number of Teachers of Color has dropped significantly, from 40% to 23%.

Another chronic issue that continues to plague Illinois public school districts is frequent teacher turnover. Teachers coming into a school and leaving after only one or two years has serious consequences ranging from excessive expense for school districts, negative impact on school culture, and most disconcerting, student achievement (Phillips, 2015; Ronfeldt, Loeb, & Wyckoff, 2013). At GYO, we believe the issues of teacher turnover and a lack of diverse, community grown teachers are intimately linked. As will be discussed in greater detail, one of the factors that led to the creation of GYO was the revolving door of teachers in low-income neighborhoods on Chicago's west side. Community groups who first identified the problem struggled to find solutions. They provided induction training, "get to know the community" learning sessions and even support from more veteran teachers. Yet, they found time and time again, teachers from outside the community were not staying. The confluence of issues (i.e., poverty, segregation, lack of funding) overwhelmed the new teachers. And without a pre-existing and overarching commitment to the community, the teachers did not stay. Because GYO teachers are from communities like the ones where they end up teaching, they stick around longer and help not only defray the costs associated with turnover, but also are better able to relate to students and their parents. GYO teachers are deeply committed to teaching and making a difference in the lives of their students and they are committed to the communities where they live and teach.

WHY CULTURALLY COMPETENT AND COMMUNITY-FOCUSED TEACHERS MATTER

At GYO we believe, as the research has shown, that there is value for all students in the sheer fact of having diverse teachers in the classroom. As Dr. Rogers-Ard, from the Oakland Unified School District has argued, it is both subversive and transformative for all students to witness a person of color in the front of the classroom as an authority figure who is the holder and conveyer of knowledge and power. But for students of color, the impact is even more far reaching. Not only can Teachers of Color act as role models and an inspiration for students of color, but they significantly impact student outcomes. Recent studies have shown black teachers are more likely than white teachers to recognize black children as gifted (Grissom & Redding, 2016). Further, Black teachers expect more from black students, particularly black boys, than white teachers do (Gershenson, Holt, & Papageorge, 2016). These studies alone establish the very real positive impact on the achievement, academic outcomes, and self-esteem Teachers of Color can have on students of color.

At GYO, beyond just being diverse, we believe teachers need to be community focused. They need to have a familiarity with, and commitment to, the communities where their schools are situated. The community driven aspect of the program is often overlooked and undervalued. It has been our experience that many in the field of education underestimate the need for not just culturally competent teachers, but community centered and focused teachers. To illustrate the importance of understanding the context of a community in order to successfully reach and teach high needs students, the public education landscape in Chicago today and 15 years ago, when GYO was just emerging, will be explored.

THE SOCIOPOLITICAL CONTEXT OF EDUCATION IN CHICAGO

Chicago has been, and remains, one of the most racially segregated cities in the country (Frey, 2015). Its public school system reflects that segregation and is made worse by economic segregation that concentrates large numbers of low-income children of color in underfunded schools on the city's south and west sides. These same students who are facing segregation and under-resourced schools, are also living in the midst of an epidemic of gun violence. As of June 2016, more than 1,500 people have been shot and 270 have been killed. This violence is concentrated in the same areas as the under-resourced schools. The context in which students live and are educated matters and having teachers trained in and familiar with these realities is critical. For GYO, understanding the complex dynamics in a neighborhood are as vital as diversity. Understanding this background is necessary to understand why GYO was created and why it is still so needed today.

THE START OF GYO

One of the characteristics that makes GYO most unique among teacher training programs is its roots in, and continued connection to, the community. It was born out of the work of community organizations that were struggling to find qualified teachers who could serve their urban schools for the long term. In one Chicago neighborhood, North Lawndale, the local community organization, ACORN (now Action Now) tried several means of enticing and attracting the best and the brightest of teachers from across the state, but teachers from outside of Chicago rarely stayed in the schools or the community. The impact of the constant teacher turnover was felt by the students and the school community as a whole. In another neighborhood on the Northside of Chicago, Logan Square, the culture of the school was not keeping pace with the changing demographics of its students. The neighborhood had an increasing Latino immigrant population, yet the administration and faculty of the local schools were predominantly white, English-only speakers. The cultural mismatch between the students and their teachers was negatively impacting student performance, morale, and parent engagement. Though different issues, both resulted from a lack of culturally competent, community focused teachers who were in it for the long haul.

The program that served as the catalyst for GYO, the Parent Mentor Program (PMP), was housed in the Logan Square Neighborhood Association (LSNA). LSNA developed the PMP as one means of addressing the cultural disconnect between students and teachers. PMP places parents in classrooms for a few hours each day to support teachers and students. The Mentors are provided intensive training prior to entering the classroom and receive rigorous on-going training throughout the program. The program made a huge difference in bringing the culture of the students and their families into the school. While participating in the program, some Parent Mentors fell in love with being in the classroom and teaching students. They wanted to do more, they wanted to become teachers. But, for many, the prospect of returning to school after years away and finding the time and means to finance their education seemed impossible. Out of their passion came a pilot project called Nueva Generación. LSNA partnered with local university Chicago State and together they secured a federal grant to provide a path for a small group of dedicated and passionate parents to become teachers.

While the Parent Mentor Program flourished, ACORN continued to struggle with teacher retention. Realizing the issue was larger than one neighborhood, ACORN created the Chicago Learning Campaign (the Campaign) to examine issues plaguing public schools across Chicago, with a special focus on teacher quality. The first organization invited to become part of the Campaign was LSNA. ACORN members were invited to visit students in the Nueva Generación program and learn more about the process of becoming a teacher. The members were excited about the possibilities presented by the program and wanted to bring the same opportunity to community members on the west side of Chicago. Sensing that developing talent from within the community could address many issues, such as teacher quality, retention and cultural competence, the Chicago Learning Campaign decided to expand Nueva Generación across the city and the state.

Recognizing the need of communities beyond Chicago for committed, culturally competent teachers, the GYO founders sought to enshrine an expanded Nueva Generación program into state law. They believed passing a state statute would be the most effective tool for institutionalizing and expanding the program, as well as, securing stable funding from the state. Culling the most successful aspects of Nueva Generación and integrating input from experts in teacher training, the Chicago Learning Campaign crafted a bill that after much effort and organizing became the Grow Your Own Teacher Education Act in 2004. The first year of passage the bill did not have any appropriations attached, but the following year, the campaign successfully fought for funding and secured a $1.5 million planning grant. The planning grant was used to develop GYO collaborations across the state. To better reflect the statewide scope of the work and to create an institution committed to the expansion and administration of the program, the Chicago Learning Campaign became a separate non-profit organization they named Grow Your Own Illinois.

Grow Your Own Teachers grew from the seeds of Nueva Generación and eventually became a statewide program to provide an opportunity for community members who are passionate about education and their neighborhoods to become teachers. GYO did not grow overnight from a small pilot project to a state wide program; it was developed into one by the thoughtful and strategic planning of a group of committed community organizations. Its roots in organizing are one factor that sets it apart from other teacher training programs and ensures it retains its focus on social and racial justice.

THE GROW YOUR OWN TEACHER EDUCATION ACT

The Grow Your Own Teacher Education Act (the Act) outlines almost all aspects of the program. It details the structure of a GYO partnership, the eligibility criteria, requirements for candidates once admitted to the program, the supports candidates should receive while in the program and requirements of candidates once they graduate. The Act requires that the program be administered by collaborations among diverse partners referred to as "consortia." Each consortia consists of a community organization, a higher education institution and at least one public school district.

Together consortia identify and screen potential teacher candidates that meet rigorous standards and show promise as potential teachers. The statute requires that potential candidates be a parent, a para educator, a community leader or any other individual from a community with a hard-to-staff school. Candidate's must hold a high school diploma or its equivalent, have experienced an interruption in his or her college education, exhibit a willingness to be a teacher in a high needs school, with the goal of maintaining academic excellence, and show an interest in postsecondary education. In 2014, as part of an effort to expand the pool of eligible candidates, GYO advocated and won changes to the statute to allow candidates with college degrees into the program. The hope was by allowing career changers into the program, one of the common critiques of the program, length of candidates' time to graduation, could be addressed. Unfortunately, soon after the law was changed, the state entered into a protracted budget battle that led to a year plus without a state budget. During that time all state appropriations were on hold and GYO placed its recruitment efforts on-hold until additional funding was secured. As a result, absent the recruitment of candidates with degrees, we have been unable to determine the impact in the change in the law.

GYO TEACHERS: THE RECRUITMENT PROCESS

Having its roots in the Parent Mentor Program meant GYO's main candidate pool was, and continues to be, adults. The majority of GYO candidates are low-income working parents. 74% of GYO candidates are women, 71% have dependents and 86% work either full or part-time. They are returning to school after a long hiatus or entering a higher education classroom for the first time. For many, the dream of returning to, or starting college, had been elusive.

Potential GYO candidates come from many places, but the close connections GYO community partners have within their neighborhoods provide ample opportunities for outreach and recruitment. In a typical candidate selection process, representatives from the partner organizations work together to review application materials including a written essay, references and any prior college transcripts. Once candidates pass the initial screening, an in-person interview is scheduled. The interview is held with multiple partners at the table, including GYO coordinators, higher education partners, current GYO candidates or teachers, and principals or staff from the local school district. During the interview process potential candidates are asked to discuss their interest in teaching, their commitment to academic excellence and their commitment to community. Candidates are asked if they are affiliated with any community organizations, if they have been involved in their local schools and what, if any, work they have done with children in the past. If the consortium determine the prospective candidate has the potential to succeed, the candidate is invited to participate in the program. Acceptance into the GYO program is contingent upon acceptance into the partner higher education institution. In some cases, new candidates are not ready for the university and may be admitted to the program on a probationary basis. During the probationary period, prospective candidates will take community college courses and attend community events, but do not receive any financial support.

GYO TEACHERS: THE PREPARATION PROCESS

Once admitted, the candidate must adhere to the academic standards of GYO as well as those of the higher education institution. The candidate signs a contract stating he or she understand the terms and conditions of the program. The GYO program requires candidates to maintain a 2.5 GPA, to attend monthly cohort meetings at the community organization, and once they graduate, to teach in a qualifying school position for at least five years. Regularly scheduled cohort meetings, when candidates come together with their GYO coordinator, are a time when candidates can share issues they are having academically and emotionally. These meetings augment the curriculum they receive at the university level and provide candidates an opportunity to build relationships with each other. Curriculum for the cohort meetings vary by consortia, but foundational to all is leadership development training and exploration of social justice issues impacting their communities.

Through the years, GYO has developed and refined its processes for monitoring and assisting candidates in their academic progress. Regular communication between the higher education and community based coordinators enable early interventions when issues arise. Consortia partners work together to find the best possible student teaching placement for candidates and upon graduation, the relationships consortia members have in the community, particularly their relationships with neighborhood schools, help to ensure job placement for graduates.

Historically, GYO consortia have received funds from the state, administered by the Illinois Board of Higher Education (IBHE), to provide forgivable loans to it candidates. GYO also provides candidates financial support for the cost of books, fees, tutoring, and when the funds are available, stipends for child care, transportation and student teaching. The wrap-around services that candidates receive are crafted with their unique needs in mind. Without these supports, many candidates would never make it to graduation. Beyond the financial supports, often equally important are the emotional supports candidates receive. There are GYO coordinators either at the community organization or the university to offer this support. The close collaborations between the community organizations and the university ensure candidate success during their time in school. The program is designed to ensure candidates have on-site support at the university, as well as, in the community. Because of the unique needs of GYO candidates and because of the complexity of the program, close collaboration is critical. These partnerships are a key component of GYO's success.

GYO TEACHERS: PLACEMENT AND RETENTION

Upon graduation, consortia partners work together to find graduates jobs. Because our teachers are highly qualified and come with the extra value of being from the communities and committed to staying, they are sought after by principals. GYO has a job placement rate of 87% across the state. Since the first GYO candidates graduated, the program has provided professional development sessions to continue their education beyond graduation and hone their teaching skills. GYO has worked with its higher education and school district partners, as well as local teachers unions, to create sessions, but also to direct graduates to all available professional development resources to ensure their success.

As the number of graduates began to significantly increase, in 2015 GYO implemented a pilot project to provide a more comprehensive set of supports for its graduates. The pilot program explored longer-term professional development sessions, a mentor program and more opportunities for socializing and networking. The stand-alone professional development sessions were designed and created in coordination with GYO graduates, higher education partners and school district partners. The sessions covered topics and skills that were relevant to what teachers face on a daily basis. For instance, in 2015 and 2016 topics included how to succeed within the teacher evaluation system used in their district, techniques and tools to improve classroom management, and ways to integrate literacy into all subject matters.

Two longer term projects were also launched in 2015. The first, the Inquiry to Action Group (ITAG), had as its goal the creation of a self-directed learning space for teachers to come together, decide on a topic of study and spend a protracted period (6–8 weeks) studying the topic and developing a plan of action to implement what was learned in their classrooms. We found that projects that required a lengthy commitment and multiple sessions over a protracted period, were challenging for our teachers to attend. Born out of the lessons of the ITAG, we launched a singular session to address the isolation and frustration often felt by Teachers of Color in predominantly white institutions. This sessions entitled, "Naming and Addressing Racial Battle Fatigue," was aimed at providing teachers and teacher candidates not only a safe space to discuss the everyday experience of being a person of color, but also a place to share and brainstorm coping strategies. These sessions were very popular and continue to be offered. The GYO Community Voices Project was also launched by Dr. Conra Gist, an assistant professor of Curriculum and Instruction at the University of Arkansas, to provide both teachers and candidates an opportunity to develop their personal narrative within the academic frame of the unique cultural capital Teachers of Color bring to the classroom. Both projects aimed to provide unique and varied experiences for our candidates and graduates to deeply engage with each other and with relevant content. But we learned that given their very busy schedules, it is difficult for them to commit to a long term project. Moving forward it was decided to return to shorter, stand-alone professional development sessions.

Given GYO's interest in creating teacher leaders, coupled with our need to advocate each year for funding, we often hold legislative training sessions to help prepare our teachers and candidates to speak to legislators about GYO. The sessions focus on the ins and outs of the legislative process, as well as, how to advocate individually and as a group for programs and issues of importance. In addition to trainings, GYO holds celebratory events throughout the year. GYO works to bring candidates and graduates together across cohorts to develop a shared identity and sense of comradery, as well as, to energize and celebrate the candidates throughout the year. Creating programming that helps retain GYO teachers in the classroom is an on-going project. Each year we examine and evaluate programming to determine what was successful and what else our teachers need to succeed.

GYO BEST PRACTICES

Through the years some practices have risen to the top as instrumental to the program's success. We have found four components to be most important for ensuring the success of candidates: (1) the connection to community; (2) the cohort model; (3) the wrap-around support services; and (4) the partnerships.

Community Connections

Integrated into everything is the program's connection to the community. It provides fertile ground for recruitment, is the staging ground and inspiration for the additional education candidates receive beyond the university classroom, deepens the experience and teaching of higher education partners, and helps in job placement for graduates. GYO candidates are often recruited by partner community organizations and already have some experience working in the community. They may be a leader in their community organization and fought for or advocated on behalf of a myriad of issues impacting their neighborhoods. They may have been part of the Parent Mentor program, working in a classroom and learning first-hand about the challenges students face, and the realities of working in underfunded schools in low-income communities of color. Their experiences working in the community provide important leadership development opportunities and relationship building skills, both of which are critical to engaging students and their families.

As detailed in prior sections, the issues impacting the neighborhoods where our candidates and teachers live inform the curriculum and topics of the cohort meetings. But it is not only GYO's curriculum that has been informed by the community. In fact, GYO's higher education partners will testify that their engagement with community organizations through GYO has informed not only the way they teach, but what they teach to their students. These collaborations are literally changing the landscape of teacher education at some universities. Teaching in high needs schools requires preparation beyond the four walls of a college campus. GYO candidates not only receive high quality teacher education, but they benefit from the lessons learned in a community setting about the challenges and strengths that lie in every community. They learn about the facets of the community that will shape the learning and living environment their future students will face. Practically speaking, GYO's community connections also provide ready avenues for recruitment and job placement. Relationships that community partners have with schools and principals are invaluable for recruiting quality candidates already working in schools (like security guards or paraprofessionals) and staying informed about job openings.

Lastly, the community connection keeps GYO grounded in issues of social, economic and racial justice. The work of the community organization is constantly informing the curriculum of cohort meetings and keeps GYO staff, candidates, graduates, as well as higher education partners, up to date on the issues that are impacting low-income communities of color. This awareness of issues and felt connections to the community ensure all of GYO is constantly working against the forces that collude to negatively impact communities of color and the students living in those communities.

Cohort Model

Another key aspect of the program is the cohort model. GYO's cohort model is non-traditional because it is based on geography and neighborhood rather than year in school. GYO candidates are grouped with others based on where they live. They meet monthly with their peers at the community organization and discuss not only academic issues, but also take part in additional learnings that are specific to their neighborhood. They may discuss issues like the foreclosure crisis, the lack of affordable housing, the school to prison pipeline for students of color, the closing of mental health clinics, or the epidemic of gun violence in their neighborhoods. Leadership development is a key piece of the curriculum as GYO wants its teachers to see themselves as leaders and agents of change within their classrooms and schools.

In addition to the curriculum, candidates find significant support in their cohorts and often refer to them as their "second family." Given the full lives GYO candidates have, balancing school, family and work can be overwhelming. The support of peers can make all the difference. GYO candidates can struggle with certain subjects when returning to college after years away. Their difficulties can be frustrating and disheartening and again, it is often the support of their peers that helps them persevere.

Graduates carry with them this sense of family that was created while they were students and continue to support the candidates that come after them. For instance, GYO graduate, Dimas Hinojosa, is now a high school math teacher, but he continues to attend monthly cohort meetings and inspire candidates who are still in the program. Hearing about the struggles candidates were having with math, Dimas volunteered to hold weekly math tutoring sessions on Sundays to help candidates get up to speed in their classes and to help them prepare for state-mandated tests. Further, GYO teachers are always sharing news of open positions at their schools in hopes of helping recent graduates find positions. At one school, the principal is so impressed with GYO teachers, that anytime he has an opening he reaches out to GYO. Today he has five GYO teachers.

Wrap-around supports

Built into the cohort model are the wrap-around supports that were designed specifically to aid in the success of non-traditional students. GYO aims to support and educate the whole person and that requires recognizing the unique needs of our candidates. As working adults with families to support, GYO candidates bring with them a wealth of experience and wisdom, but also many pre-existing commitments that if not recognized and honored can be obstacles to their education. To that end, GYO provides support for the cost of books, child care, transportation, and stipends during student teaching.

Partnerships

The key ingredient that keeps the program running and everything working smoothly is the strength of the partnerships. Partnerships come into play at every stage of the program. As mentioned earlier, the relationships community partners have with principals and neighborhood schools provide a great resource for recruitment, but so too do the school-based programs run by many GYO community partners. Once recruited, the admission of candidates relies on input from multiple partners to ensure a good fit for the program and the field of teaching. Supporting candidates through the program is absolutely a team effort of both the community partners and higher education partners. Just today a community coordinator was working with a higher education partner to design the best and most effective test preparation plan for one of the candidates. Navigating the university and avoiding stumbling blocks requires support at both the community level and the university level. Similarly job placement relies on partnerships in the community and with the school district. Close collaboration with school districts ensure GYO knows what positions are in high need and how to navigate hiring practices to ensure as smooth a transition from graduation to job placement as possible. Finally, GYO's work and collaboration does not end with job placement. GYO continues to partner with school districts to develop professional development sessions that align with district priorities and policies. Further, GYO partners with local teacher unions to provide additional support to graduates. Whether that be asking the union's assistance in pairing recent graduates with more veteran teachers in their school or taking advantage of the high quality professional development sessions offered by the union, collaborating with local union affiliates has enormous benefits for teachers. Each partner brings a diversity of opinions and experience to the collaboration that makes the hard work of recruiting, training and retaining diverse, community focused Teachers of Color possible. It is hard to imagine the program being successful without each partner at the table.

GYO TEACHERS AND CANDIDATES

In their own words, the following section features some GYO candidates and teachers sharing the impact the program had and continues to have on their success.

GYO Candidate, Fatima Salgado

> I'm a native Chicagoan, but my parents moved to Mexico when I was 2 or 3 and I first went to school in Mexico. When we moved back to Logan Square, I needed English language support in school and didn't get it until the end of 2nd grade. I watched "Arthur" cartoons on TV every day and repeated every single word. That was my support. I won third place in a Young Authors contest for a story about how difficult it was to not be able to communicate.
>
> I had a male teacher for the first time in middle school, a math teacher. He was very inspirational. He really pushed me. Another male teacher encouraged me in science. He felt that more women should be in science.
>
> I went to Hubbard High and was in the IB (International Baccalaureate) program, the boy's swim team, track and field and volleyball. Later I wound up at Hancock. I took all honors classes and ended up with a 4.0 GPA.
>
> All the colleges I applied to, I got accepted. I didn't get enough financial aid so I started at City Colleges, at Daley, going to school full-time and working part-time as a security guard. In October of 2012, I got a call from a Hancock counselor who told me about a part-time tutoring position at Castellanos Elementary.

I got placed with a first-year teacher. Three students needed language support. Without any formal training, I took on that responsibility and created lesson plans for them. I felt like I didn't know what I was doing, but at the same time I realized that I liked it and that I really liked teaching. The kids were learning and beginning to speak English in short sentences. They inspired me to become a teacher.

The teacher who I worked with was a Grow Your Own graduate and he told me about the program. I applied and got in November 2014 and I transferred to Northeastern.

Grow Your Own wants us to have hands-on experience with our communities and I've been very active with Telpochcalli School. The more you know about what's happening outside the school, the more you can understand what's happening with students inside the classroom.

I expect to graduate in 2017. I've been working as a special ed assistant for two years at Castellanos and the principal wants to hire me. I want to coach track. I prefer middle school. I want to teach science and math.

Grow Your Own has been a great resource —whenever we have questions, they always have help on the table. It's dedicated to the candidates and teachers who have gone through the program. I also think it is well-rounded—they take the candidates as a whole and use their strengths. My strength is athletics. Since I coached sports that helps me more than a psychology book or theory to reach students.

Financially, Grow Your Own has been the best support. I hate talking about the possibility of the program losing funding. Grow Your Own works. You're going to take away the one thing that will help us complete our education? It's ridiculous. I've done a lot in my 21 years of life to earn my bachelor's degree. And I'm battling for the money to stay in school and finish? I don't deserve that and my fellow candidates don't deserve it. I see it on their faces. They're worried. I'm worried, too.

It's not just about us or our tuition. It's about knowing how to prepare students in our community. They need to have a strong foundation. Many of them are constantly told "No, you can't do that." We candidates are all going to create a safe and cultural classroom environment where the students feel safe and know they are worthy as human beings. Classrooms lack that now.

Linda Wilson, GYO 2nd Grade Teacher

The Peoria School District has 14,000 students, and about 55 percent are African American. But only 6.7 percent of teachers are African American. We have a growing population of Latino students and we have a huge need for male teachers. We need more diversity in our district.

I'm interested in helping the effort to increase minority recruitment and bringing back the Grow Your Own Teachers program is one way to get more diverse teachers in Peoria classrooms.

I am a graduate of Grow Your Own Illinois. I applied and got into the program in 2008 when the program was launched here. I was a teacher's aide at the time. I had been in school at Illinois Central College, but just taking classes here and there.

Grow Your Own encouraged non-traditional students to pursue careers in teaching. For me, it was a godsend. Before getting in, I had no idea how I was going to complete my degree. I didn't know if I was going to have to beg and borrow from family members. While I was going through the program, I was surrounded by supportive peers and mentors. There were other people who were like me and had some of the same challenges—juggling school, families and jobs. It really helped us bond.

There were so many components to the program that were helpful. I traveled to Chicago for the statewide networking meeting and heard Stanford University professor Linda Darling-Hammond speak. I networked with other teachers across the state. I got training and leadership development. With the stipend and forgivable loans, I was able to go full-time to Bradley University, where I got my bachelor's in early childhood education.

Since I graduated, I've been teaching 2nd grade. I'm going into my fifth year at the same school. My school is three blocks away from my house. I see students and parents on my block and at the grocery store. I'm really invested in my community and my students.

We have a lot of people who go to Bradley to become teachers and who student teach in Peoria schools and then go back to Chicago. Teachers in Peoria schools live in surrounding communities. There's nothing wrong with that. But you see things through a different lens when you live here *and* work here.

I've lived in Peoria all my life and attended public schools here. My husband and I have five children.

Recently, there was an open invitation to the community to attend meetings and share their ideas about how to improve Peoria schools, and one discussion point was that Peoria needed more minority teachers. When I read about it in the local newspaper, I talked about it with our Local 780 president. He recognizes the need for more diverse teachers here and understands what Grow Your Own can bring to our school district.

I read an article about how white children benefit from having Teachers of Color. I'm a black woman. I have a career. I have a family. Some of our students—poor black and poor white students—don't go beyond a six block radius of their homes. We are a river town and some kids have never seen the river.

For children who don't have resources, it's important for them to see a black teacher. There aren't many of us and students need to see a variety of black teachers to dispel stereotypes.

I'm working to bring Grow Your Own back to Peoria. The community wants great teachers and Grow Your Own produces quality teachers. We have high GPAs. We continue our education by pursuing masters' degrees. We are invested in the communities and teaching children inside and outside the classroom. We are making sure students learn and that they are successful.

Grow Your Own opened doors for me, and created possibilities that did not exist for me before the program was around. I went from being a young mother to becoming a teacher with two master's degrees. I know there are others who want to become teachers but who—like me—just need a few doors opened and some encouraging words.

Jacqueline Croffett, GYO Special Education Inclusion Teacher

I spent a lot of time volunteering at schools when I had two sons growing up. I was a teenage mom, and we kind of grew up together.

I was volunteering at a middle school when one of the lead parents asked me if I'd ever thought about becoming a teacher. I said no. She said she thought I'd be good and told me about Grow Your Own.

There was a parent group, and I became the parent liaison with the district. I was sent to a No Child Left Behind conference in Chicago, and it was awesome. It was a turning point for me. I learned about standards and curriculum and the need for teachers. I learned about the No Child Left Behind law. People shared personal stories. It touched me. I wasn't really aware until then about how many kids were behind and missing the mark. I also learned that there were not enough of us, African American teachers, to meet the needs of students.

When I came back from that conference, I submitted my application for the Grow Your Own program. I started with Grow Your Own during 2008 and went to Southern Illinois University in Edwardsville. It was hard. There were a lot of days I wanted to quit. The classes were tough and trying to go to school full-time and work part-time in home health care and raise kids—it was hard. Grow Your Own provided the childcare, the books, the tuition. My cohort, my crew, we encouraged each other. My colleagues got me through. We developed life-long relationships. I came in with some credits from working on an associate's degree, and I graduated in 2011 and I've been teaching ever since.

There's a lot more to teaching. It's not just ABCs and 123s. It's life. And I have to understand where students are coming from. I grew up here. I was a teenage mom myself. I see them at the grocery store and on the block. I can relate to them. It makes all the difference in the world. They don't sit down and talk to strangers. They have their guard up. So I watch. I listen. I wait for an opening. I have been where they are.

My first job was co-teaching 10th grade English Language Arts. I was there for a year. The next year I was laid off. I was out of a job for the following year. I worked for summer school programs. Then I came back and was employed as a special education teacher. I'm currently co-teaching special education. I love it. I work primarily with 5th grade and I'm a resource teacher for 3rd grade.

I would describe Grow Your Own as personable, supportive and relational. I think about the relationships and connections I formed with my cohort group. I'm close to them. We're always touching base here and there. We were always there to support each other.

GYO CHALLENGES

Through the life of the program we have encountered many challenges ranging from selecting the right candidates, helping candidates pass required high stakes exams, and diversifying funding sources for the program.

GYO Candidate Selection

When the program first began there was a much more open and inclusive approach to admissions. A consequence of this approach was the admission of candidates that ultimately could not complete the program and led to a high attrition rate. Though retention is challenging for all higher education programs working with non-traditional students like ours, the program acquired a reputation for having an unusually high attrition rate. In response, for the last few years we have refined our admissions processes and requirements and began looking more closely at a candidate's likelihood of success. To that end, some consortia instituted a pre-GYO program that provides a period of observation of potential candidates prior to full admission. Some consortia have found that many potential candidates are passionate about education and committed to their community, but not yet ready to make the leap to GYO. If a candidate is designated for Pre-GYO, he or she joins a GYO cohort and they are expected to play an active role by attending monthly cohort meetings and participating in other GYO activities, but they take classes at the community college level without any financial support from GYO. This provides the potential candidate a glimpse at both the rigors and supports of GYO. If the potential candidate succeeds academically and shows a high level of participation in the cohort, if space is available, he or she is invited to join GYO and receive the full range of GYO social, academic, and financial supports.

State Teacher Certification Exams

Related to the issue of attrition and academic readiness is the challenge GYO candidates have had passing the state mandated test required for admittance into any college of education in Illinois. Failure to pass the Test of Academic Proficiency (TAP) prevents otherwise eligible students from entering the College of Education. For some GYO candidates, the combination of test anxiety and years away from the classroom, results in a failure to pass the TAP. It is important to note GYO candidates are not alone in this struggle. According to the Illinois State Board of Education website, in 2015, only 17% of Hispanic test takers and 14% of African American test takers passed, compared with 37% of their white counterparts.

This test has been an issue for years and GYO waged a statewide advocacy effort to change it. Its disparate impact on students of color directly impacts the number of new Teachers of Color across Illinois. GYO continually hears from frustrated superintendents and principals from across the state about the small hiring pool of available Teachers of Color. There simply aren't enough. The desire is there, but there are simply not enough Teachers of Color graduating from colleges of education across the state to meet the demand. And that shortfall can in part be attributed to the test that determines who is able to enter into colleges of education.

The first iteration of the test, the Basic Skills, had a similar impact on students of color, and through much effort on the part of GYO and allies across the state, some progress was made. GYO waged a state wide effort that began with the building of a coalition of allies that included students who had failed to pass the test, university faculty, school districts administrators and legislators all of whom understood the negative impact the test was having on communities of color. The coalition talked to countless legislators and held many hearings. Eventually, GYO's advocacy efforts resulted in the lifting of the number of times the test can be taken (it is not now unlimited) and it was determined that the ACT plus writing could be taken in lieu of the TAP. Despite these changes, and the fact there is no demonstrable connection to teacher quality, the test continues to be a significant road block to future Teachers of Color. After GYO's organizing efforts to change the test, GYO switched its focused to better preparing candidates for the test. GYO provides candidates intensive test preparation boot camps coupled with individualized tutoring. Modest gains have been made, but the work continues. Long term, the fight against the test needs to be revisited and work needs to be done to implement a better measure of a candidate's aptitude to be a teacher.

Diversifying Funding

Perhaps the biggest lesson we have learned is one we are currently facing head on. Since GYO's inception, the programmatic pieces of GYO have been funded by annual state appropriations. Each year GYO must advocate for a new appropriation. The state funding has been a boon, but not one without significant challenges. The nature of annual appropriations, which are determined by the sometimes fickle Illinois General Assembly, is one of uncertainty. It makes planning for the future nearly impossible, and requires an inordinate amount of time and resources advocating for funding. Beyond the usual vagaries and uncertainty of state appropriations, for the last 15 months Illinois has been held hostage by the battle between the Republican Governor and the majority Democrat General Assembly. They have been unable to reach an agreement on a budget and the state went without a budget for over a year. During the summer of 2016, there was a patchwork stop-gap budget passed, but many social service agencies were not included. Consequently, many state programs, GYO included, have gone without state funding over a year. Though extraordinary, the budget impasse highlights the need to diversify funding. This is a problem not easily solved, but one that must be addressed to ensure the long term sustainability of the program.

CONCLUSION

What we have learned is that training community-focused Teachers of Color is very hard work that requires a great deal of time and resources, and an enormous commitment. It is not work that can be completed absent a deep and abiding commitment to training and retaining Teachers of Color. The work is challenging, in part because the higher education system and teacher training programs were not designed for students like ours. It was designed for "traditional students," which more often than not means young people who just graduated from high school and are entering college with the financial and moral support of their parents, most of whom themselves graduated from college. But the majority of our students, and many college students for that matter, are different. They are adults, they work, they have families and they bring with them a lifetime of rich and meaningful experiences. But often they don't have the resources to help them navigate an alien and sometimes hostile educational environment. This is where GYO comes in. We understand and value all of the aspects of our candidates' lives. In fact we think their differences are actually their strengths. We think the things that set them apart are the same things that will make them amazing and inspiring teachers who will be able to transform the lives of their students. Until our education systems shift to meet the needs of all students, GYO will work to ensure there are opportunities and supports for those amazing people who want to spend their days changing the lives of students who are most in need.

REFERENCES

Boser, U. (2014). Teacher diversity revisited: A newstate-by-state analysis. *American Center for Educational Progress*. Retrieved from https://cdn.americanprogress.org/wpcontent/uploads/2014/05/TeacherDiversity.pdf

Frey, W. (2015). Census shows modest declines in black-white segregation. *Brookings institution*. Retrieved from https://www.brookings.edu/blog/the-avenue/2015/12/08/census-shows-modest-declines-in-black-white-segregation/

Gershenson, S., Holt, S. B., & Papageorge, N. W. (2016). Who believes in me? The effect of student–teacher demographic match on teacher expectations. *Economics of Education Review*, *52*, 209–224.

Grissom, J. A., & Redding, C. (2016). Discretion and disproportionality. *AERA Open*, *2*(1), 1–25.

King, M. S., Kan, L., & Aldeman, C. (2016). *Who's teaching our kids: Changes to Illinois' educator workforce since 2002–2012*. Retrieved from http://bellwethereducation.org/sites/default/files/Bellwether_IL%20Educator%20Workforce_16_0702_0.pdf

Phillips, O. (2015). Revolving door of teachers costs schools billions every year. *National Public Radio*. Retrieved from http://www.npr.org/sections/ed/2015/03/30/395322012/the-hidden-costs-of-teacher-turnover

Ronfeldt, M., Loeb, S., & Wyckoff, J. (2013). How teacher turnover harms student achievement. *American Educational Research Journal*, *50*(1), 4–36.

GYO Illinois Commentary

NICHOLAS MICHELLI

This chapter on "Grow Your Own Illinois" is an example of a successful partnership in Illinois among colleges and universities, communities, and the State of Illinois to not only enhance the diversity of teachers for the Chicago Public Schools, but to successfully recruit individuals from the communities they will serve. In the 10th year of its existence, 2016, GYO has prepared 118 teachers with 91% Teachers of Color and 86% teaching in high needs schools in their communities. The chapter reports successes and continued challenges in meeting the needs of Illinois and bemoans that it still has work to do after a decade. Why is this important and what exactly is the problem? Why does diversity continue to be a problem? What must our society do to solve the mismatch between the racial and ethnic identity of teachers and the students they teach?

It is in some ways amazing that we label this effort a success—and we do and should. But, with all the effort and success reported, the contribution has been 118 teachers out of a 20,567 teaching force—surely a drop in the bucket in an effort to diversity teachers in the Chicago Public Schools (Chicago Public Schools, 2016). In this commentary I consider what the diversity (or lack of it) is, why this effort is important, what the strengths of and lessons to be learned from the GYO program are, and some of the roadblocks to even greater success in Chicago and nationally. In doing so we pay tribute to those who organize and continue this effort against significant odds, and consider what this says about our society.

IS THERE RACIAL DIVERSITY?

First, the mismatch between the racial and ethnic make-up of the teaching force and that of public schools students is undeniable and remains significantly unequal. The United States Department of Education, through its National Center for Educational Statistics (NCES) reports on the disparity regularly at the national level, and occasionally in major school districts. Reporting in 2016 nationally, the NCES found that between 2003 and 2013, the number of White students in public schools decreased from 28.4 million to 25.2 million, with the percentage dropping from 59% to 50%. The number of Hispanic students increased from 9.0 million to 12.5 million, growing from 19% of the total to 25% of the total. Black students remained at about 16% nationally (Schools and Staffing Survey, 2011–2012a).

The data were somewhat different for Chicago, where in the 2010 report, it was found that of the 396, 683 public school students, 9.4% were white, 39.3% were Black, and 45.6% were Hispanic. Comparatively, Chicago had the second lowest proportion of Black students among the 20 largest school districts, and the highest proportion of Hispanic students (Chicago Public Schools, 2016). In contrast, for the teaching force nationally, most recently reported data were 83.1% White, 7% Black, and 7.1% Hispanic. (Schools and Staffing Survey, 2011–2012b). The teaching force in Chicago was reported as 50.3% White, 22.3% African American, and 20.1% Hispanic. (Chicago Public Schools, 2016). In summary, for Chicago, the comparative percentage of teachers and students (not accounting for unidentified or mixed race) were:

Table 4.2. Comparative Percentages of Teachers and Students by Race.

	White (%)	Black (%)	Hispanic (%)
Teachers	50.3	22.3	20.1
Students	9.4	39.3	45.6

IS RACIAL DIVERSITY IMPORTANT?

The authors report some studies showing the impact of diversity in a variety of ways, but it must be noted that evidence of same race teacher impact on achievement is inconclusive at the present. In a careful review of six studies specifically examining the impact of same race teachers, Villegas and Davis (2008) found that,

> It is impossible to reach any definitive conclusions about the merit of teacher diversity polices based on the six studies examined ... All six studies suffer from some sort of

> limitation … (and these studies) provide no insight into the underlying mechanisms by which teacher race/ethnicity influences student learning. (p. 587)

Villegas and Davis note that, as women of color, they know the impact of Teachers of Color on their own education. As researchers, however, they have sought empirical evidence of the impact. After an extensive review of the literature, they conclude by saying that "we are now convinced there is sufficient evidence to suggest that teacher race and ethnicity do matter in the education of students of color. Our review does not support a color blind perspective on the relationship between teacher and student race/ethnicity" (p. 599). This conclusion by these two researchers, among the best examining the issue and supporting culturally responsive teaching, is evidence to me that the work is indeed important and that research on the mechanisms of impact need to continue. It should be noted that this important line of research has in fact continued since the Villegas and Davis 2008 publication. There are additional studies, including Grissom and Reading (2016), Easton-Brooks (2014), Eddy and Easton-Brooks (2011), and Egalite, Kisida, and Winters (2015). Still more work is needed. Although we may never find incontrovertible empirical evidence of a connection between same race teachers and their affect on the learning of students, each of these studies add at least to the evidence base on the importance of diversity.

Villegas and Davis also examined other impacts of diversity in schools, including studies demonstrating that the assignment of students of color to special education was inversely proportional to the proportion of same race teachers. The more Teachers of Color present, the less likely students of color were classified. Perhaps most convincingly, there is evidence that student self-concept is enhanced by the presence of a successful same-race teacher in the classroom. I would argue further that this has to do with what Maxine Greene has said about the failure of schools when she reports that, "We cannot become what we cannot imagine" (Greene, Personal Correspondence, 2005). What better extension of the imagination of possibilities for students of color than seeing a successful Teacher of Color in the classroom? We should argue that imagination and self-concept are an important outcome of these diversification efforts, too.

WHAT ARE THE STRENGTHS OF AND LESSONS LEARNED?

The author outlines the strengths of their work accurately, including a strong commitment to placement and retention. This commitment to placement is not unusual, but seems stronger than in traditional teacher education programs, and the commitment to retention is very unusual and important. Many traditional programs provide placement services for students, especially where there is a strong school university partnership. Retention is another matter that is often left to the school districts. There are few examples of teacher education programs that actively seek to enhance the retention of their graduates to the extent this program does. Teacher attrition is among the most expensive items in the budgets of urban schools, and this effort not only reduces costs, but also enhances continuity of learning. This aspect of the GYO program should be reported widely and replicated.

The program leaders also sought actively to influence policy to support their work, including working toward an act of the Illinois Legislature, The Grow Your Own Teacher Education Act, and identifying the important elements of the program. These include:

- A partnership that includes a community organization, a higher education institution, and a public school district
- Admissions requirement that candidates are from the community, hopefully as a parent, a paraeducator, or community leader.
- Requiring candidates to have a high school diploma, an interrupted college experience or a college graduate, and a willingness to be a teacher in a high needs school.

In addition, the Illinois Board of Higher Education agreed to provide forgivable loans to candidates along with support for the costs of books, tutoring, child care, and the like. These are often barriers to students of color, often coming from lower socioeconomic levels. After students are admitted a focus on continuing to meet academic standards is important. As reported, the program learned from earlier efforts that attention to the likelihood of success is important. Attending community meetings is an important learning experience that helps students understand the context from a more academic and abstract perspective allowing them to generalize. It builds on their experience in the community, but goes beyond it.

The strengths that seem most important are the origins of candidates in communities they will serve—truly "grow your own." This, along with extensive support during teacher education, seem to make success much more likely. In addition the program has, as noted, successfully sought government buy-in and policy changes.

What Are the Roadblocks to Success?

Perhaps most pervasively, a roadblock is the continued presence of racial prejudice in our society and an absence of a commitment to social justice and the acceptance of so-called minorities. I say so called minorities because we are very close to a time where there will be no majority, and one does not have minorities without a majority! I will back up this claim with just three examples, without even going to the most recent presidential election, which seemed replete with examples of prejudice. First, the author reports on the negative effect of licensure tests in Illinois on the success of candidates of color and on their success in making some changes. Much research has been done to demonstrate this bias in standardized tests generally, and for the SAT in particular. For example, Rosner (2003), cited in Au (Au, 2015) found this practice, as reported by Au:

> Each individual SAT question ETS chooses is required to parallel outcomes of the test overall. So, if high-scoring test takers, who are more likely to be right, tend to answer the question correctly in (experimental) pretesting, it's a worthy SAT question. If not, it's thrown out. Race and ethnicity are not considered explicitly, but racially disparate scores drive question selection which in turn reproduce racially disparate test results in an internally reinforcing cycle. (Au, 2015, p. 29)

This conclusion, that the SAT tests favor white students, is particularly important for teacher educators as the Council for Accreditation of Education Providers (CAEP) replaces the National Council for Accreditation of Teacher Education (NCATE). CAEP requires that teacher education students score in the top 50% of all students taking the SAT, GRE or ACT, whichever applies (Council for Accreditation of Education Providers, 2016). It is highly possible, given the finding by Rossner reported above, that this will further negatively impact the racial diversity of teacher education programs. There is no valid evidence that the use of admissions tests like the SAT and GRE predict the success of teachers. In fact, if the SAT is designed to predict student success in the first years of college, since most college programs admit students to teacher education after the first two years of study, the academic record is a far more valid bit of evidence than the admissions test. Furthermore, there is little evidence that the process of accreditation of teacher education programs has successfully pushed diversity of programs. There was indeed a standard in NCATE on diversity, but there is little evidence that diversity changed among accredited colleges (Jacobowitz & Michelli, 2008). There is no longer a standard *per se* under CAEP. Rather, diversity is seen as a "cross-cutting" theme over several standards and relevant elements of standards can be identified. However, none of these elements are among the seven elements absolutely required by CAEP for accreditation. An institution can fail to meet any of the elements said to be related to diversity and still be accredited. That implicitly says that other aspects of accreditation are more important. Furthermore, the visiting team representing CAEP on site is not required to write the quality of the evidence supporting work towards diversity. This may further diminish any further enhancement of pushing for diversity through accreditation.

Next, the replacement for No Child Left Behind, the Every Student Succeeds Act (ESSA) was signed into law in December, 2015 turning much responsibility over to the states that had been required by NCLB. As states have considered local regulations for the implementation of ESSA, in at least one case I am familiar with, the state has posed this question to a review committee: "Should our state continue its efforts to insure equity in education?" An amazing question, I thought. I would have countered with "Should our state BEGIN efforts to insure equity in education?" The bottom line is that we must monitor policy at all levels to be sure that no further erosion of a push to equity occurs. At least one other element of ESSA should be noted. The law calls for the establishment of Academies for Teacher Preparation (actually educator preparation since it includes school leaders). Under this provision the federal government could fund academies set up outside traditional colleges of education to prepare teachers. While this provision might provide an option for more programs with a clear focus on diversity, that certainly does not seem to be the intent of the law. In fact, ESSA in discussing academies, further deprofessionalizes teacher education by precluding states from requiring either a Ph.D. for faculty or accreditation for the program. The partnership model GYO uses is by far the best. Colleges can in fact apply for academy funding, and GYO might want to encourage partners to develop funded academies with an even greater commitment to diversity.

Clearly, the effort by GYO to support diversity in teacher education is an unusual commitment that is critical and must be maintained and expanded. However, we must not be complacent. Even with this evidence of the importance of the work GYO engages in, they have had to fight for continued funding to keep the program alive.

REFERENCES

Au, W. (2015). High stakes testing: A tool for white supremacy for over 100 years. In B. Picower and E. Mayorga (Eds.), *What's race got to do with it?* (pp. 21–44). New York, NY: Peter Lang.

Chicago Public Schools. (2016). *CPS stats and facts.* Retrieved from: http://cps.edu/About_CPS/At-a-glance/Pages/Stats_and_facts.aspx

Council for Accreditation of Education Providers (2016). *The CAEP Standards.* Retrieved from: http://www.caepnet.org/standards/introduction

Easton-Brooks, D. (2014). Ethnic-matching in urban schools. In H. R. Milner & K. Lomotey (Eds.), *Handbook of Urban education* (pp. 97–113). New York, NY: Routledge.

Eddy, C. M., & Easton-Brooks, D. (2011). Ethnic matching, school placement, and mathematics achievement of African American students from kindergarten through fifth grade. *Urban education, 46*(6), 1280–1299.

Egalite, A. J., Kisida, B., & Winters, M. A. (2015). Representation in the classroom: The effect of own-race teachers on student achievement. *Economics of Education Review, 45*, 44–52.

Grissom, J. A., & Redding, C. (2016). Discretion and disproportionality: Explaining the underrepresentation of high-achieving students of color in gifted programs. *AERA Open, 2*(1), 1–25.

Jacobowitz, T., & Michelli, N. (2008). What can the future be? In M. Cochran Smith and K. Zeichner (Eds.), *Handbook of research on teacher education* (pp. 479–485). New York, NY: Routledge.

Rosner, J. (2003). On white preferences, *The Nation, 276*(14), 24.

Schools and Staffing Survey. (2011–2012a). *Public school teacher data file*. Retrieved from https://nces.ed.gov/pubs2009/2009324/tables/sass0708_2009324_t12n_02.asp

Schools and Staffing Survey. (2011–2012b). *Public school teacher data file*. Retrieved from https://nces.ed.gov/surveys/sass/tables/sass1112_2013314_t1s_001.asp

Villegas, A., & Davis, D. (2008). Preparing teachers of color to confront racial/ethnic disparities in educational outcomes. In M. Cochran Smith & K. Zeichner (Eds.), *Handbook of research on teacher education* (pp. 583–605). New York, NY: Routledge.

CHAPTER FIVE

Cultivating Teachers of Color as Change Agents: A Model of Critical Race Professional Development

JOSEPHINE PHAM AND RITA KOHLI

Figure 5.1. ITOC Symbol: Create.
Source: José Ramirez

José Ramirez was commissioned to paint, *Create,* as the logo for Institute for Teachers of Color (ITOC) Committed to Racial Justice. The image reflects the intellectual engagement, community-orientation, and indigenous cultural connectivity of powerful teachers of Color who reimagine schools for students of Color.

Table 5.1. Institute for Teachers of Color (ITOC) Committed to Racial Justice Overview

Demographics	Since 2011, ITOC has served 354 teachers of Color from across the US. While teachers are admitted into the program from all over the nation, most are from California (approximately 85%), in a large part because of the burden of travel costs. Other ITOC teachers attend from across the nation (e.g. Oklahoma City, OK; Houston, TX; Chicago, IL; Baltimore, MD; New York City, NY; Atlanta, GA; Tucson, AZ; Seattle, WA; Sioux Falls; SD). ITOC teachers work in K-12 schools and are diverse in terms of race, gender, years of teaching experience, and age; specifically: • 48% of participants have been Latina/o, 20% Black, 20% Asian American and Pacific Islander, and 12% of participants identified as mixed race or other • 78% of participants have been women, and 22% men. • 68% of participants have been in the classroom five years or less, and 14% have been in the classroom ten years or more • Participants' ages ranged from early twenties to late fifties • The majority of ITOC teachers are secondary. In our most recent cohort, 30% were elementary teachers.
Funding Sources	ITOC is funded by university support and participant registration fees. The organizers and workshop facilitators serve as volunteers.
Mission	ITOC supports the growth, success and retention of teachers of Color who work in K-12 public schools serving students of Color. Framed by critical race frameworks, ITOC is intended as a community building, professional development space for teachers of Color to explore the racial climate of their schools, receive leadership training to navigate these realities, and strategize how to create racially transformative classrooms and schools.

Preparation and Timing	ITOC is an annual three-day critical professional development program, serving teachers of Color with advanced racial literacies and potential to serve as racial justice leaders in K-12 schools. A unique collaboration between the disciplines of teacher education, educational leadership and ethnic studies, ITOC rigorously selects 60- 80 teachers of Color each summer to cultivate their racial analysis and leadership capacities as educational change agents. They are presented with frameworks, resources, and models to better identify racialized issues at their school sites and strategize how to engage in transformative work and positive racial school reform. Teachers are recruited to ITOC through social media, as well as professional and academic electronic lists that include university faculty, teacher educators, educational leaders, teachers and teacher candidates. ITOC is also on faculty pages and university websites of the organizers of the conference. Despite serving a range of teachers across the pipeline from pre-service to veteran, and from diverse geographic locations where racialization manifests in varying ways, the content of ITOC is not differentiated. ITOC is a dialogical space that encourages teachers to engage across their positionalities including their race, region, age, citizenship status, gender, sexuality. Because they share an advanced racial literacy in a community oriented setting and there is space for them to apply their learning to their individual contexts, there is rarely conflict; rather their expertise is strengthened through diverse interactions. Following ITOC, teachers stay connected through social media (i.e. Facebook, twitter), and many return to the conference from year to year, as well as plan to meet at other social justice education conferences around the country such as Free Minds Free People, NYCoRE, and Teachers 4 Social Justice.

INTRODUCTION

Edna was a social justice oriented Latina enrolled in a prestigious teacher education program in the diverse Bay Area. With the goal of improving the educational conditions of her community, she was one of few teacher candidates of Color in her cohort. Edna and her peers were being trained to teach in a working class community of Color, a community to which Edna felt accountable. However, all of her professors were White and the majority of texts centered White teachers teaching students of Color, often through deficit and individualized explanations of inequality. Even the veteran teachers Edna was positioned to learn from were entirely White and rarely justice driven. Edna felt racially and ideologically isolated from her own education. She was not exposed to frameworks or teaching practices that matched her professional goals or identity, and she felt ill equipped to create transformative educational opportunities for her students.

Like Edna, many teachers of Color choose teaching because they want to improve the academic experiences of students of Color (Irizarry & Donaldson, 2012), support the educational transformation of their own communities (Dingus, 2008), and act as racial justice advocates (Perry, Steele, & Hilliard, 2003). Compared to white teachers, practicing teachers of Color have more positive views of students of Color, including more favorable perceptions of their academic potential and higher expectations for their learning (Boyle-Baise & Sleeter, 2000; Dee, 2005). Often because of personal experiences with culturally disconnected curriculum, or the under-resourced conditions of their schooling, teachers of Color also tend to have a heightened awareness of educational injustice and racism (Irizarry & Donaldson, 2012). And while there are teachers of Color who do not engage in discussions of injustice, existing research demonstrates that teachers of Color are more likely to frame racist and classist experiences within a broader socio-political context (Kambutu, Rios, & Castañeda, 2009).

Despite the potential that teachers of Color bring to classrooms to address racial inequity and improve the educational opportunities for students of Color, as in the case of Edna, teacher education programs tend to neglect their experiences, perspectives and needs (Amos, 2010). Studies have revealed that not only is most teacher training devoid of any structural or racial analysis of inequity (Gorski, 2009), it is also designed primarily for white teacher candidates (Montecinos, 2004; Sheets & Chew, 2002). Teacher candidates of Color are often ignored and silenced within classes, and stunted in their professional growth (Amos, 2010; Parker & Hood, 1995). Practicing teachers of Color have also reported feeling isolated, unsupported and overlooked for leadership opportunities at their school sites (Dingus, 2008; Kohli, 2016). Additionally, very little professional development addresses issues of social injustice, let alone racial inequity or racism (Cochran-Smith & Villegas, 2015). Teachers of Color, who are recruited into schools for racial equity minded reasons, are typically not mentored, supported, or even allowed by school staff to do racial justice work (Phillips & Nava, 2011).

But what could happen if teachers of Color were developed in ways that built upon their positionality, perspectives and social justice goals? If Edna and other justice-oriented teachers of Color were exposed to frameworks that strengthened their critical racial analysis of schooling, would they be better equipped to improve the educational conditions of students of Color? How might they be positioned to reimagine education for students, for communities and for themselves?

With the rise of scripted and skill based teacher professional development (PD), teachers are rarely offered space to develop their critical analysis of inequity (Zeichner, 1993), and are thus increasingly ill positioned to have any agency to challenge the status quo (Giroux, 1988). Critical theory, and in particular Critical Race Theory (CRT), is rarely introduced to teachers (Solorzano & Yosso, 2001), but we argue it has tremendous implications for a teacher's ability to identify and challenge racial injustice in schools. In this chapter, we share a program portrait of the Institute for Teachers of Color (ITOC) Committed to Racial Justice, a CRT guided intensive professional development program, to demonstrate how teachers of Color can be positioned as racial justice leaders in urban schools. We begin by describing the dimensions of ITOC, including the structures, the theoretical framework that guides praxis, and a model to illuminate the pedagogical elements involved in ITOC. We then share examples of three case studies from ITOC teachers who, equipped with a critical race analysis and tools for action, created educational spaces that support on-going critical teacher development for themselves and their peers. Following the analysis of these case studies, we then discuss how the model of ITOC addresses gaps in traditional teacher development. Finally, we conclude with recommendations for educational leaders to (re) design or remodel programs to better center the needs and leadership potentials of teachers of Color.

DIMENSIONS OF THE INSTITUTE FOR TEACHERS OF COLOR COMMITTED TO RACIAL JUSTICE

Structure

ITOC emerged as a response to growing restrictions in teacher education that limit critical and racial justice discourse (Gorski, 2009), and as a support to the often-overlooked needs of teachers of Color (Montecinos, 2004). A unique union between teacher education, educational leadership, and ethnic studies, ITOC annually brings 60–80 teachers of Color from across the country together to engage in three days of community building, professional growth, and racial justice leadership development. ITOC differs from many other social justice teacher development spaces because there is a selective application process used to facilitate an intimate learning environment of exceptional educational leaders, much like a cohort based teacher education program. Selected teachers must exhibit an advanced racial literacy (Skerrett, 2011), engage in an asset framing of communities of Color (Yosso, 2005), and actively apply critical theory to their practice (Camangian, 2010). ITOC then facilitates a community of racial justice minded teachers of Color who use CRT to deconstruct structural racism, challenge deficit belief systems, and build upon the rich knowledge of their communities to transform schools.

CRT Praxis

CRT emerged in the 1970s from critical legal studies, ethnic studies and women's studies to illuminate institutionalized racism as a key barrier in US racial reform (Bell, 2004; Delgado & Stefanic, 2013; Ladson-Billings, 1998). An interdisciplinary theory, CRT challenges ideology, policy and practice that use individualized explanations for racial inequality such as colorblindness and meritocracy. The theory has been adapted into various disciplines, and became part of the landscape of critical educational scholarship in the late-1990s to draw attention to the conditions of racial inequality in K-16 school contexts (Ladson-Billings, 1998; Solórzano, 1997).

Over the last two decades, the impact of CRT research in education has grown tremendously (Ledesma & Calderón, 2015), identifying critical issues such as the educational pipeline crisis (Yosso, 2005), racial microaggressions (Solórzano, Allen, & Carroll, 2002), and hostile campus racial climate (Jayakumar, Howard, Allen, & Han, 2009). Today the theory has solid footing in the field of education (Ledesma & Calderón, 2015), yet, critics and CRT scholars alike have identified the need for more application (Crenshaw, 2010; Leonardo, 2009), reminding us that the purpose of CRT is not simply to understand racial power, but also to change it (Sleeter, Neal, & Kumashiro, 2014). Solórzano and Yosso (2001), more specifically, have called for teacher education programs to engage CRT, yet there are few models and little research to date about the use of CRT in the preparation or development of teachers. In this chapter, we illuminate how applying CRT to professional development of teachers of Color can better position them to challenge structures of racism at their school sites.

Critical professional development is an emerging framework to provide social justice oriented teachers alternative spaces to develop their critical consciousness in relation to their professional goals (Kohli, Picower, Martinez & Ortiz, 2015; Picower, 2015). Bridging CRT to critical professional development, ITOC is designed to provide teachers of Color with a critical race analysis alongside the tools to advance educational justice. Conceived out of a workshop held at several social justice teacher conferences that provided teachers of Color a separate space to discuss racial inequality and its impact on themselves and their students, it was clear how rare and necessary racially insular spaces were for teachers of Color to engage in a structural critique of racism and its impact on communities of Color. Thus, the decision was made to expand this workshop into a larger national conference.

A MODEL OF CRITICAL RACE PROFESSIONAL DEVELOPMENT

Through traditional models of teacher education, teachers are rarely equipped with complex language, constructs or applied theories that are crucial to transforming education. The teachers of Color that attend ITOC already have a self-identified commitment to justice and an advanced racial analysis that is steeped in their history, community experiences, and professional lives. To further illustrate how ITOC bridges their political commitments to their professional context, we describe the intersections between CRT-guided learning context and curriculum, and how they interact in order to deepen their critical racial literacy (Sealey-Ruiz, 2011). Such a model illuminates the possibilities of critical race professional development and its abilities to reframe teacher leadership capacities to advance racial justice (see Figure 5.2).

Learning Context

Primary to the success of ITOC in developing teachers of Color as racial justice leaders is that it is a racial affinity space that fosters complex, safe and healing conversations about the intense racialization that they experience professionally. Many teachers of Color expressed a need for support and models of racial justice praxis in schools led by people who reflected their positionality, thus all "experts" in the space leading these conversations are also people of Color. Additionally, ITOC intentionally selects speakers and workshop leaders who encourage the difficult conversations traditional professional development shies away from and facilitate cross-racial connections between participants that strengthen their racial analysis.

ITOC is also structured to foster community. Recognizing that the racial and ideological isolation critical teachers of Color experience in schools contributes to their attrition, they not only need tools to challenge racism, but they need to see themselves part of a broader community of change agents. Team building exercises and working group sessions to dialogue about specific school contexts allow ITOC teachers to build collaborative relationships with like-minded colleagues.

Curriculum

Through theory driven keynotes and workshops on topics such as anti-Blackness, intersectional oppression, the school to prison pipeline, and liberatory pedagogy, ITOC teachers are engaged as critical intellectuals who identify, understand and challenge racial inequities that exist in K-12 schools. They are also exposed to models of non-violent communication, restorative and transformative justice, community building and self-care, that are designed for them to use with students, but are also tools to support their own professional growth, well-being and retention.

In addition, ITOC teachers are guided to address specific issues of racial inequity at their school sites. Teachers of Color, who bring incredible potential to schools, are often overlooked or silenced (Amos, 2010). Because they are not typically equipped with tools to navigate the racially hostile climates of K-12 schools, they often face resistance to ideas and goals that challenge the status quo (Kohli & Pizarro, 2015). To move beyond reactionary or individualized methods of intervention, ITOC prompts teachers of Color to systematically understand the issues at their school sites or districts. In large working groups, they are engaged to consider a pressing issue of racial inequity that they want to address during the following school year. They are asked to reflect on theories or models in the conference that speak to their concerns. With a partner or in a small group, they are then asked to assess the issue; they must answer: who is involved, what is the root cause, what are the barriers to change, who are your allies in this work, what resources do you need, what must you learn to transform the condition? Next, they create a plan for action that includes a timeline and ways to collect evidence of change. Sometimes they work with teachers from their school sites or local districts, and sometimes it is teachers from other cities who are working to address similar issues. The actions of ITOC fellows have included developing a social justice track at their school site, educating colleagues about racial microaggressions, and what we focus on in this chapter, constructing on-going critical development opportunities for themselves or their peers. At the end of these projects, not only have teachers of Color made lasting impact in their schools or districts, they report feeling more confident and empowered as leaders.

ITOC TEACHER OF COLOR ACTIONS

ITOC impacts the individual teachers of Color who attend, but also has broader affects on schools and students. To highlight these positive impacts, we share three case studies of ITOC teachers who, selected through purposeful sampling, served as change agents by supporting the critical development of teachers at their school or in their community. Diverse in race, ethnicity and the type of work they engage in, each of the fellows was from the Bay Area, California and attended one or more ITOCs from 2013 to 2015.

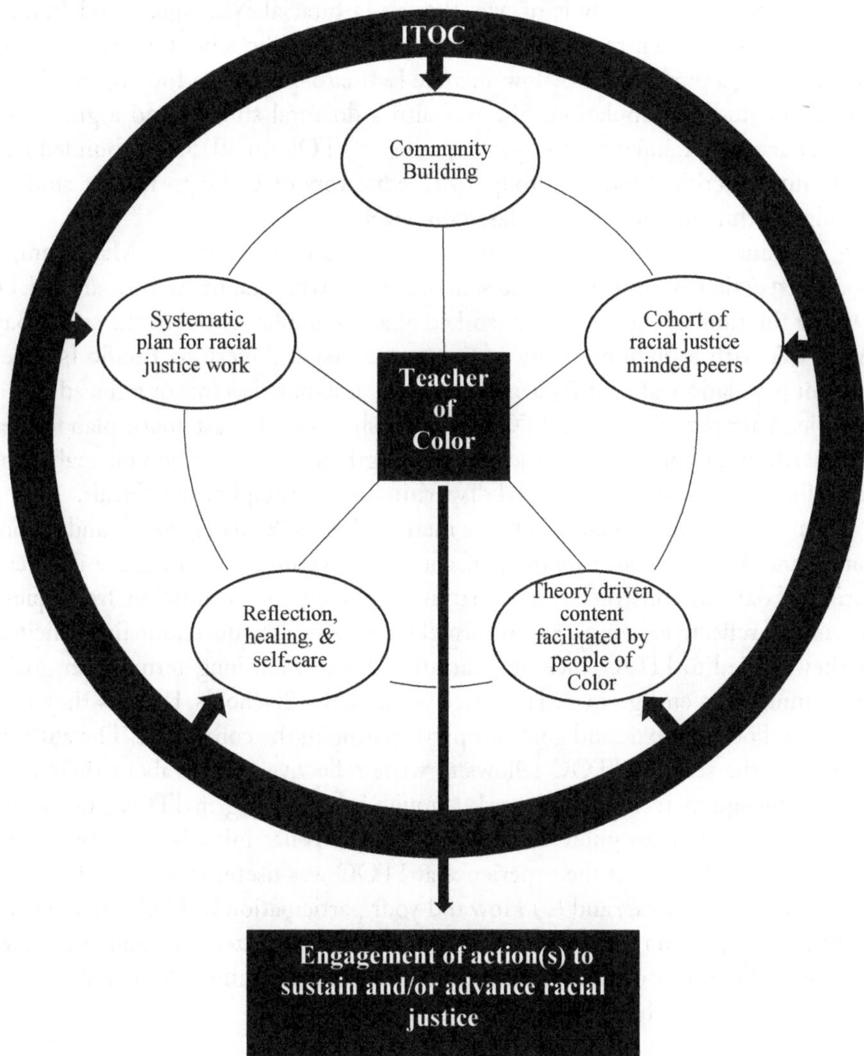

Figure 5.2. Model of Critical Race Professional Development.

The first case study we present is Mr. Ramirez, who identifies as a stateside Chamorro, Pacific Islander with roots on the island of Guam. He taught high school English at a large comprehensive high school in the south Bay Area, serving a predominantly working class Latina/o and Asian American Pacific Islander student population. As a result of his participation in ITOC in 2013, he co-created a teacher support network with two other ITOC fellows who also taught in the south Bay Area to sustain their long-term racial justice commitments.

The second case study is of Ms. Patricia, a biracial Nicaraguan and Iranian bilingual kindergarten teacher. She works at a K-6 public school in the East Bay Area, serving a predominantly low-income Latina/o, American Indian, and Asian American student population. She was also a doctoral student and a grassroots teacher activist/organizer. After participating in ITOC in 2015, she founded and co-facilitated critical inquiry groups with educators of Color to impact student learning within and beyond the classroom level.

The final case study we present is about one of the authors, Ms. Pham, a Southeast Asian American middle school teacher who taught English and ELD. During the time of the study, she worked at a 6–8 public school in the south Bay Area, CA with a predominantly Latina/o and Asian American Pacific Islander student population, almost 70% of which were designated as free or reduced lunch eligible. After participating in ITOC in 2013, she created a systematic plan for her school site and implemented an action to strengthen teachers' structural analysis of schooling in order to address racial disparities in the disciplinary referrals.

Building on traditional qualitative methodologies (Saldaña, 2015), and Solórzano's and Yosso's (2002) method of counterstorytelling, we integrate different forms of data to construct counternarratives including information from questionnaires, reflective memos, and informal interviews. The questionnaire, solicited as they applied to ITOC, included narratives about their long-term career goals, opportunities to engage in racial justice work in K-12 schools, barriers they face in their school contexts, and goals for participating in the conference. The authors also asked the selected ITOC fellows to write reflective memos about their abilities to engage in racial justice work through participating in ITOC, using the following questions to guide their responses: (1) What initially brought you to ITOC?; (2) What about the experience at ITOC was useful to your professional context or experiences?; and (3) How did your participation in ITOC shape your abilities to engage in racial justice work? Finally, we conducted informal interviews as a form of member checking to clarify experiences and actions conveyed in their written responses (Merriam, S. B., & Tisdell, E. J. (2015).

Case Study 1: Mr. Ramirez

Although Mr. Ramirez attended a social justice oriented teacher education program, he did not have a formal space to continue conversations about racial justice in his professional context. Realizing that ITOC centered the positionalities of social justice oriented teachers of Color, Mr. Ramirez was inspired about the possibility of participating.

> I remember sitting in my classroom one late evening. I received the emailed application from ITOC and it felt like I received some esoteric correspondence from an underground group of superheroes. I could tell by the questions being asked in the application process

> that this was a movement to raise consciousness and activism amongst teachers of Color. The mere thought of "Professional Development" that openly discussed racial justice was so foreign to me at the time. I mean, racial justice was on my mind constantly in schools but there weren't any spaces "sanctioned" within the teaching day. At that time, I could speak only with the few trusted colleagues when the doors and windows were closed, or when we were safely out of earshot from other folks who did not share the same values about racial justice.
>
> So, receiving the invitation to apply to ITOC meant to me that there was actually a space dedicated to building community while working through the racial injustices experienced on the daily in school settings. Aside from community spaces, or spaces within my social justice oriented teacher education program, these spaces did not exist for me. I wasn't plugged in and I didn't feel safe talking about racial justice at school. Without tenure, or without an environment that fostered these conversations about racial justice, I felt unsafe discussing the issues I was thinking about most deeply. I knew I needed to immerse myself in a space that not only validated my thinking, but that would also challenge my thinking about racial oppression as through the lens of schooling.

Mr. Piseas' initial reactions to ITOC, described as "foreign" and "underground" work, highlights the ideological isolation he was experiencing as a teacher. Alienated from like-minded teachers, he felt paralyzed in his racial justice goals. As politicized learning did not exist within his work context, ITOC felt like a needed opportunity to reengage his critical learning about racial justice work in schools.

Having a formal space to openly discuss issues of racial injustice within ITOC's learning context, Mr. Piseas was able to strengthen his racial justice teacher network and capacity as a change agent,

> The network of folks that I have connected to through ITOC has been priceless. Knowing that I can pick up the phone, send an email, or meet face to face with folks that share a commitment to racial justice is empowering because it gives me a sense of place and interconnectedness. Being able to connect with professors, teachers, and community folk with similar visions of schooling possibilities has contributed to feeling less isolated.
>
> Workshops and dialogue at ITOC have developed my capacity for understanding issues of racial justice and equity in schooling. My capacity for taking action has also grown as a result of ITOC. ITOC's specific time for developing tools to take back to our communities has been instrumental in developing as an educator. Nowhere else does this space exist—a place where tools for racial justice can be learned, adapted, and critiqued all within the span of three days. The ITOC process has allowed me to see myself as a more active educator working towards racial justice, social justice, and educational equity.

The intersections between learning about racial justice and community building with a cohort of like-minded peers galvanized a sense of collective identity for Mr. Ramirez. This served as a catalyst for mobilization to sustain his commitment to racial justice work in community.

Having time during ITOC to create a systematic plan for racial justice work, Mr. Ramirez developed goals to continue building with his peers beyond the professional development opportunity. One example included collaboration between Mr. Rameriz and an ITOC fellow who also worked at his school site.

> I had known Victoria prior to ITOC yet our relationship as colleagues has flourished since. ITOC allowed us to foster a shared language and understanding of the inequities we experience on the daily as teachers of color, working with students of color from working class families. Victoria and I are now next-door neighbors at the same high school in East San Jose and we have been able to collaborate on curriculum, Professional Learning Communities, and overall daily support as a result of the relationship forged at ITOC.

Furthermore, he mobilized a larger network of teachers beyond his schooling context by developing critical inquiry groups with other ITOC teachers who worked at other schools in the same city and community.

> Mike and I had both worked together prior to ITOC, yet after developing ideas during our ITOC work sessions, our vision of creating an alternative Professional Development space based on Teacher Inquiry Groups solidified. While our "Critical Friends" group does not exist solely for the purpose of racial equity work, the work is interconnected to the struggles to end racism and oppression through our classroom pedagogy. During our gatherings, we build in a similar supportive fashion to ITOC, by developing, discussing, and critiquing pedagogical tools, methods, and theories that allow us to engage in liberatory praxis.
>
> Understanding the potential for our work across the district we started recruitment and scheduled our 1st monthly meeting in August. Since that time in August, we've met once a month throughout the school year with the purpose of growing together as educators dedicated to meeting the needs of our students. Collectively our experiences with "Professional Development" were inadequate in their lack of awareness around issues of race, class, gender, and violence. The space we created brought much-needed fulfillment and affirmation to the participants involved. At a monthly meeting there are usually anywhere from 5–10 educators present. There have been 6 different Inquiry presentations where educators have taken on self-selected issues of importance, researched and presented those inquiries using the "Critical Friends" protocol. This month we'll be gathering in a more celebratory mood, in order to "build community through art."

Reflecting on his abilities to engage in ongoing racial justice work, Mr. Ramirez shared the value of ITOC on his as well as his peers' professional growth as racial justice leaders.

> Culturally responsive, racially conscious, and effective Professional Development will come rarely, if ever, from district mandates. [We must center] the conversation back to [what was said] at ITOC: "We are the ones we've been waiting for."

ITOC's learning context and curriculum strengthened Mr. Ramirez's critical ideas about self-efficacy, which fostered the co-creation of a fluid, collaborative space to sustain his and his colleague's own critical development needs. Through their shared actions, they were able to build a teacher network in their own community to continue developing and refining anti-racist pedagogy. This teacher network served as a crucial component of their sustenance as racial justice leaders and practitioners as they are able to work as critical teachers through self-guided study.

Case Study 2: Ms. Farima

While Ms. Farima served and participated in other social justice-oriented teacher professional development and networks, she had never engaged and learned with teachers of Color exclusively. She applied to ITOC, excited to develop her knowledge and skillsets in this racial affinity context.

> I was drawn to ITOC because I am a grassroots organizer within a social justice teacher organization and work closely with other educators of color, but I had been wanting to have a people of Color exclusive space to talk about and develop my own analyses on critical theories and frameworks to inform my practice on a deeper level. I continue to find myself frustrated at the lack of time or opportunities to discuss these issues at schools with my colleagues. Navigating multiple education spaces (graduate school, K-12 teaching, and grassroots organizing), I find myself feeling overwhelmed and in need of support to sustain critical conversations, solidarity work, and love. Unfortunately, this space is not common in formal institutional spaces, therefore, it becomes increasingly difficult for me to feel a sense of belonging and value in public education.

Ms. Farima came to ITOC deeply committed to her work, as evident in her multiple roles as a classroom teacher, graduate student and grassroots teacher organizer. She expressed a need for nurturing spaces to foster her professional growth, given the weight she carried in all of these roles. Thus, reflection, healing and self-care became a pivotal aspect of her experience in ITOC, particularly the ability to discuss stressors that impacted her experiences as a teacher of Color.

One key example was her learning about microaggressions through Solórzano's (2015) keynote presentation.

> It was so helpful to be provided with a theoretical and research-based presentation on my lived experience working in predominantly White spaces. I always wondered if the feelings I felt when being on the receiving end of microaggressions were just me being overly sensitive or even dramatic. His presentation helped me to trust myself and understand that I'm not alone in those feelings, especially as I engaged in conversations with other teachers of Color about it after his talk. It was validating on a lot of levels.

Not only did these frameworks affirm her personal experiences, they helped her reframe these experiences through a structural lens. Learning about microaggressions, along with other concepts such as community cultural wealth, racial battle fatigue, and schools as sites of Whiteness (Burciaga, Pizarro, & Kohli, 2015) deepened her analysis of structural inequalities and expanded possibilities of her work as a teacher scholar activist.

> [The keynotes] really helped me to understand why I was having (and still experiencing) anxiety attacks and mental health issues because of the constant feelings of surveillance, policing, micoraggressions, stereotype threat, and so many other issues that I carry every single day as an educator and graduate student of color. Yolanda Sealey-Ruiz's keynote [about self-care and healing] was what got me to realize that I needed to engage in healing as a form of radical love that I could and should engage with my educator of color friends and community. All of these elements helped me to reimagine my work as a teacher organizer of color and inspired me to create a new space for teacher empowerment, development and healing.

Seeing the power of spaces led by and for teachers of Color, one of the core components of ITOC's learning context and curriculum, Ms. Farima wanted to create a formalized space for justice-oriented teachers of Color who were seeking critical development. Ms. Farima contacted the founder of her grassroots organization, hoping to develop a critical inquiry group specifically for educators of Color, using CRT and Yosso's (2005) Community Cultural Wealth as frameworks to guide their conversations.

> During our organization's annual retreat I shared my ITOC experience with the group, and I explained how empowering it was to have a people of Color exclusive learning space. So often teacher learning spaces feel like silos, centering conversations with classroom teachers and excluding the voices of other people of Color who also impact the learning of students of color. I wanted this critical learning space to be open to educators of Color, broadly defined, i.e. including community/afterschool educators, professors, juvenile hall/prison educators, resource specialists, administrators, etc. I decided to start a study group, centered and driven by educators of Color. This study group is intended to build on the leadership strengths, critical analyses, racially diverse experiences/ testimonios, and pedagogical creativity of classroom and community based educators who are committed to working in solidarity with students and communities in under resourced, culturally and linguistically diverse schools in the Bay Area.

Inspired by ITOC's model, Ms. Farima engaged in an action to develop a racial affinity space for teachers of Color within a predominantly white grassroots social justice teacher organization (Pour-Khorshid, 2016). Comprised of twelve participants diverse in terms of professional work and life experiences, the study group met once a month for two hours in Fall 2015. Receiving an email from one of the participants about the possibility of extending the inquiry group for another year, Ms. Farima recognized how the teacher development space was sustaining in the same way ITOC sustained her.

> I've been co-facilitating this educator of Color space [with two other teachers of Color] since the beginning of the academic year and it has been amazing and transformative. The

> fact that these teachers come to this space faithfully after work on their own time AND want to extend their experience for another year is amazing to me. Even more than that, the folks in this group are also taking ownership of our space by bringing in what they believe will support them in their own growth as critical educators of color. This particular educator who sent me this email identifies as a trans person of Color and has expressed how difficult it is to work with teachers at their school where they work, so much so that they feel silenced most of the time. However, they don't feel like that in our space, they even expressed how our space allows them to feel like they can breathe and heal collectively with the rest of us.

As a result of the space Ms. Farima created, the participating educators of Color were able to develop as critical leaders, equipped with CRT frameworks and newfound sense of empowerment.

Describing how participating in ITOC shaped her abilities to reimagine racial justice work with these educators of Color, Ms. Farima said the following:

> Initially, the study group was inspired by what I took away from my own personal experience at ITOC because I felt the urgency to create something that would sustain that feeling for myself, BUT it's even more incredible that I'm clearly not the only person who feels this way. This was something that the rest of our group desperately needed, too.

Ms. Farima's abilities to heal and reclaim her role as a teacher committed to racial justice sheds light on the need for racial affinity spaces and the utility of CRT in teacher development. Ms. Farima was not only in a more empowered position as a racial justice teacher leader, she built upon what she learned to construct a space for other educators of Color to unpack and challenge structural inequities that negatively impact communities of Color, sustaining their collective struggle for racial justice.

Case Study 3: Ms. Pham

Despite Ms. Pham's goals to advance educational opportunities for students from her home community, neither her teacher education nor her professional development prepared her to address and/or transform inequitable schooling.

> I lacked the language and theoretical frameworks to describe the majority of my educational experiences as a first generation college student and English language learner. It was not until I was accepted into a social justice oriented teaching preparation program that I was immersed in a world that allowed me to articulate the social injustices and inequity that I had experienced as a student.
>
> While I felt empowered in my learning, I knew that my specific needs as a teacher who wanted to teach in her home community were not being met. As one of the few teachers of Color in my program as well as on a predominantly white teaching staff, I realized more than ever that I was not white. Even when researching support for myself as a teacher of

> color in a predominantly white staff, most studies I found were about how to support white pre-service teachers in urban schools. I continued to self-advocate and seek the support I needed, although I could not name what this support would look like.

As one of the few teachers of Color in her program and on her staff, Ms. Pham's experiences were often ignored or overlooked. Her narrative reiterates the importance of a racial affinity space, as outlined in the model of ITOC, to address her unique needs. By chance, a teacher friend sent her an email that included an application to attend ITOC,

> Prior to attending ITOC, almost every mentor, professor, and administrator that I had in my teaching experiences were White. Although I learned a lot from these allies, ITOC was the first time I was within a community of teachers of Color who could speak to my experiences navigating an overwhelmingly White profession. In more ways than one, I found a space where I no longer had to mold myself to fit into an existing structure—I could reimagine what it meant to be a teacher and what it meant to teach for social justice. Building community within a group of like-minded teachers was both healing and reviving at the same time. Having peers who have engaged and were currently engaging with related issues in different contexts spurred me to learn from their experiences in order to reflect, plan, and implement action within my own school context.

Ms. Pham had learned about racial justice with like-minded peers before, but this was the first time the dialogue spoke to her specific positionality as a teacher of Color. Such an experience spurred her abilities to re-imagine her own role and reframe her students' schooling experiences with a critical lens.

> While participating in ITOC, I learned critical frameworks that enabled me to sharpen my analysis and strengthen my ability to both name and challenge inequality, including racial microaggressions, racial battle fatigue, counternarratives, and community cultural wealth. These frameworks were particularly helpful for me in reframing the frameworks for positive student behavior at my own school site. While the data revealed that our school site had average referral rates compared to the national average, there was a disproportionate amount of Latino and Black males who received referrals. This was further exacerbated through my peers' assumptions that students came from tough home environments and did not care about their education. Knowing that my students' experiences and voices did not align with these dominant narratives, I used the critical frameworks I learned to develop an action plan that aimed to challenge deficit thinking and reduce campus discipline measures.

Like Ms. Farima, the concepts Ms. Pham learned at ITOC were essential to her abilities as a teacher leader. But rather than building with like-minded teachers, she decided to engage in critical development with colleagues at her school site. With the goal of systematically shifting discipline practices at her school site, Ms. Pham challenged the colorblind narrative used to frame campus climate at her school site using data-driven practices that unveiled racial disparities.

Presenting her systematic plan to her administration after ITOC, Ms. Pham implemented her action the following school year to address the disproportionate number of students of Color impacted by school-based punishment.

> Identifying individual students with high referral and suspension rates, predominantly comprised of Black and Latino males, I conducted student focus group interviews, organized by grade level and gender. I presented transcriptions of these focus group interviews to my peers in a staff development. Using counterstorytelling to reframe student perspectives and experiences, the narratives revealed how and why students were negatively impacted by top-down, deficit approaches to discipline, challenging previous assumptions of academic underachievement and disengagement of students of color.
>
> Teachers were able to make sense and interpret concrete evidence of student experiences, as well as were able to define, self-reflect, and challenge deficit discourse. They were also able to identify examples of racial inequality and its systemic impact on the status and experiences of the students from the data. Counterstorytelling allowed teachers to experience a more holistic narrative of the student experiences, enabling them to connect student responses about their schooling experiences to their motivation and life experiences. This holistic narrative helped teachers to consider factors that contributed to the root of the problems instead of making generalizations about the student's "problem behavior" in itself. In light of this collective analysis of the counternarratives, teachers met in grade level teams to discuss and reframe their own disciplinary practices. By the end of the school year, referral rates reduced by almost 30% compared to the year before.

Guided by CRT, Ms. Pham's action challenged deficit perspectives about students and strengthened teachers' structural analysis of schooling through staff development, engaging teachers (white and non-white) at various levels of racial literacies in conversations about students' racialized schooling experiences. Using students' counternarratives as a way to develop peer teachers' critical perspectives on schooling, Ms. Pham was able to enact change within the formal institution of school. Shifting the school culture in this way enabled her to establish allies within her school, as she now had colleagues who challenged institutional barriers and teacher action as a means to improve the educational experiences of students of Color.

What she learned at ITOC galvanized her plan and action to advance racial justice at her school site. Ms. Pham reflected,

> I came to understand my personal experience as more than just an isolated, personal story; it was what my ITOC fellows and I represented in the grand scheme of hegemony in education.

Not only did ITOC support her abilities to name and challenge deficit frameworks that negatively impacted her students' schooling experiences, ITOC helped her understand the power of building on the critical analyses of teachers of Color and repositioning them as change agents in the education system.

DISCUSSION

Given the overwhelming presence of whiteness in teacher preparation (Sleeter, 2001), teachers of Color are rarely offered frameworks that build upon their positionalities and interests, even in the context of social justice-oriented spaces. Teachers of Color, who many times work in colorblind contexts and are racialized, are also often overlooked and undervalued for leadership work (Kohli, 2016). Because of the many restrictions and current framings of teacher education, teachers get very little training that points to structural causes from inequity, offers language or tools to navigate racism in schools, or provides space for critically conscious teachers to grow deeper in their analysis or transformatory goals.

The ITOC model is an important intervention in the traditional preparation and development teachers of Color receive. The three teachers in these case studies all expressed feeling unsupported, isolated or under-equipped to accomplish their racial justice goals before they attended the summer training. Within ITOC they were exposed to critical theory within a community of like-minded teachers who were striving for justice in schools. In this space they were intentionally developed and reframed as racial equity leaders in schools. These components helped them to feel self-empowered; as Mr. Ramirez referenced one of the keynotes—they were finally able to see themselves as the leaders they had been waiting for (Burciaga, 2014).

Prior to ITOC, many teachers who attended did not have a space to discuss issues of racial injustice or an affinity space for people of Color to discuss their racialization. Participants expressed that these circumstances limited their abilities to realize their racial consciousness on the ground (Knight, 2002). ITOC helped to translate the existing racial justice goals of teachers of Color into action. More specifically, these case studies were examples of teachers of Color using frameworks, tools and community they gained from ITOC to create transformative teacher development spaces in three distinct ways: Building with like-minded peers, collectivizing teachers across a city, and reframing deficit thinking within a school site. Each of the teachers of Color highlighted in the case studies being engaged in racially transformative leadership work, and facilitating the critical development of other teachers. Doing so enabled them to reshape curriculum, pedagogies and frameworks that positively impacted students, schools and communities.

ITOC functions as a racial justice teacher development program that repositions teachers of Color as mobilizers of educational justice. Without a critical framework to interpret race and class based inequality, the pervasive and unexamined impetus that oppressive institutions have on students of Color will continue to misframe their experiences as underachieving and disengaged. Instead, ITOC supports teachers to implement CRT driven actions that can shift school structures and teacher discourse from the marginalization of communities of Color to building upon their cultural wealth. As evident in the three case studies, teachers of Color were able to transform educational opportunities through peer teacher development inside and outside schooling institutions.

RECOMMENDATIONS

For teachers of Color to take leadership in this work of reframing systemic inequity, there are key things that must be in place for their development. Teachers of Color carry the baggage of U.S. racialization into their role as educators. They have been told within their own education and their professional roles that they are inferior, that their opinions and voice do not matter as much, and they have been stripped of power—even in schools within their own communities. To begin to develop teachers of Color as the racial justice leaders they deserve to be, the first step must be one of healing. This healing can come from being in a community of like-minded people, from being educated through knowledge and frameworks that center their epistemologies, and from developing literacy for the mechanisms of racism that are used to oppress communities of Color. This healing can both strengthen their critical consciousness to recognize and name racism, as well as offer them tools to thwart an internalization of racism. Teachers of Color must also be provided with tools, opportunities and encouragement to use their critical consciousness and deep, personal understanding of oppressive institutions to lead racial justice interventions. We realized that teachers can only grow so much when exposed only to models to how schools currently exist. To support teachers reimagining the possibilities of schooling, teachers must be exposed to frameworks that exist in other fields such as ethnic studies, women and gender studies, psychology, social work and community organizing. When this is formalized and collectivized, teachers of Color feel self-efficacy as leaders to transform education, and in the case of these case studies, the capacities of their peers. Teachers who engage in this type of development have shared that they not only feel empowered to tackle the very challenging work that they have set out to do, but they also feel "rejuvenated," "motivated," and that being part of this community towards change has prompted them to persist in the profession. As Berenice, a 14th year high school humanities teacher, shared after attending ITOC the second year,

> Each time, I have left with new ideas, new connections, I have entered battered and exited put back together—no longer questioning my own sanity. No longer feeling alone and isolated—at peace with the struggle that always awaits me after the summer and strengthened by the love and commitment that these like-minded people show.

Teacher education programs must make space for the kind of self-reflection and critical structural analysis we see in ITOC. Teacher educators and school leaders must be able to see the assets teachers of Color bring into schools, and center their experiences, beliefs and goals. Borrowing from the model of ITOC and the teacher of Color leadership outlined here, programs can make space for community building, including emphasis on restorative and transformative justice. Teachers also need space to process their experiences as teachers; self-care and critical frameworks are an essential component of recognizing and naming their humanity. Programs can also consider recruiting and retaining critical educators of Color as role models for this work as well as provide leadership tools to cultivate transformative thinking and transformative work. This may take shifts in the epistemological approaches used to further develop teachers as socially conscious change agents. However, if we are going to better support students of Color in schools, critical professional development cannot only exist outside of traditional and formal spaces. Alongside this grassroots work, we must also be able to reimagine the formalized structures that shape the foundation of teaching.

REFERENCES

Amos, Y. T. (2010). "They Don't Want to Get It!" Interaction between minority and white pre-service teachers in a multicultural education class. *Multicultural Education, 17*(4), 31–37.

Bell, D. (2004). *Silent covenants: Brown v. Board of Education and the unfulfilled hopes for racial reform.* Oxford University Press.

Boyle-Baise, M., & Sleeter, C. E. (2000). Community service learning for multicultural education. *Educational Foundations, 14*(2), 33–50.

Burciaga, R. (2014). *Critical race feminiso (re)visions of school leadership. [Powerpoint slides].* Presented in San Jose, CA.

Burciaga, R., Pizarro, M., & Kohli, R. (2015). *Institute for teachers of color keynote presentations [Powerpoint slides].* Presented in Los Angeles, CA.

Camangian, P. (2010). Starting with self: Teaching autoethnography to foster critically caring literacies. *Research in the Teaching of English, 45*(2), 179–204.

Cochran-Smith, M., & Villegas, A. M. (2015). Framing teacher preparation research: An overview of the field, part 1. *Journal of Teacher Education, 66*(1), 7–20.

Crenshaw, K. W. (2010). Twenty years of critical race theory: Looking back to move forward. *Connecticut Law Review, 43*, 1253.

Dee, T. S. (2005). A teacher like me: Does race, ethnicity, or gender matter? *American Economic Review, 95*(20), 158–165.

Delgado, R., & Stefanic, J. (Eds.). (2013). *Critical race theory: The cutting edge* (3rd ed.). Philadelphia, PA: Temple University Press.

Dingus, J. E. (2008). "I'm learning the trade": Mentoring networks of Black women teachers. *Urban Education, 43*(3), 361–377.

Giroux, H. A. (1988). Teachers *as intellectuals: Toward a critical pedagogy of learning.* Wesport, CT: Greenwood Publishing Group.

Gorski, P. C. (2009). What we're teaching teachers: An analysis of multicultural teacher education coursework syllabi. *Teaching and Teacher Education, 25*(2), 309–318.

Irizarry, J., & Donaldson, M. L. (2012). Teach for America: The Latinization of U.S. schools and the critical shortage of Latina/o teachers. *American Educational Research Journal, 49*(1), 155–194.

Jayakumar, U. M., Howard, T. C., Allen, W. R., & Han, J. C. (2009). Racial privilege in the professoriate: An exploration of campus climate, retention, and satisfaction. *The Journal of Higher Education, 80*(5), 538–563.

Kambutu, J., Rios, F., & Castañeda, C. (2009). Stories deep within: Narratives of U.S. teachers of color from diasporic settings. *Diaspora, Indigenous, and Minority Education, 3*(2), 96–109.

Knight, M. G. (2002). The intersections of race, class, and gender in the teacher preparation of a Black social justice educator. *Equity & Excellence in Education, 35*(3), 212–224.

Kohli, R. (2016). Behind school doors: The racialization of teachers of color in urban public schools. *Urban Education,* 1–27. Retrieved from: http://journals.sagepub.com/doi/abs/10.1177/0042085916636653

Kohli, R., Picower, B., Martinez, A., & Ortiz, N. (2015). Critical professional development: Centering the social justice needs of teachers. *International Journal of Critical Pedagogy, 6*(2), 7–24.

Kohli, R., & Pizarro, M. (2015). Fighting to educate our own: Teachers of color, relational accountability and the struggle for racial justice. *Equity and Excellence in Education, 49*(1), 72–84.

Ladson-Billings, G. (1998). Just what is critical race theory and what's it doing in a nice field like education? *International Journal of Qualitative Studies in Education, 11*(1), 7–24.

Ledesma, M. C., & Calderón, D. (2015). Critical race theory in education: A review of past literature and a look to the future. *Qualitative Inquiry, 21*(3), 206–222.

Leonardo, Z. (2009). *Race, whiteness, and education.* New York: Routledge.

Merriam, S. B., & Tisdell, E. J. (2015). *Qualitative research: A guide to design and implementation.* John Wiley & Sons.

Montecinos, C. (2004). Paradoxes in multicultural teacher education research: Students of color positioned as objects while ignored as subjects. *International Journal of Qualitative Studies in Education, 17*(2), 167–181.

Parker, L., & Hood, S. (1995). Minority students vs. majority faculty and administrators in teacher education: Perspectives on the clash of cultures. *Urban Review, 27*(2), 159–174.

Perry, T., Steele, C., & Hilliard III, A. (2003). *Young, gifted, and black: Promoting high achievement among African American students.* New York, NY: Beacon Press.

Phillips, D. K., & Nava, R. C. (2011). Biopower, disciplinary power, and the production of the "good Latino/a teacher". *Discourse: Studies in the Cultural Politics of Education, 32*(1), 71–83.

Picower, B. (2015). Nothing about us without us: Teacher-driven critical professional development. *Radical Pedagogy, 12*(1), 1–26.

Pour-Khorshid, F. (2016). HELLA: Collective Testimonio that Speak to the Healing, Empowerment, Love, Liberation, and Action Embodied by Social Justice Educators of Color. *Association of Mexican American Educators Journal, 10*(2).

Saldaña, J. (2015). *The coding manual for qualitative researchers.* Thousand Oaks, CA: Sage.

Sealey-Ruiz, Y. (2011). Dismantling the school-to-prison pipeline through racial literacy development in teacher education. *Journal of Curriculum and Pedagogy, 8*(2), 116–120.

Skerrett, A. (2011). English teachers' racial literacy knowledge and practice. *Race Ethnicity and Education, 14*(3), 313–330.

Sheets, R. H., & Chew, L. (2002). Absent from the research, present in our classrooms: Preparing culturally responsive Chinese American teachers. *Journal of Teacher Education, 53*(2), 127–141.

Sleeter, C. (2001). Preparing teachers for culturally diverse schools: Research and the overwhelming presence of whiteness. *Journal of Teacher Education, 52*(2), 94–106.

Sleeter, C. E., Neal, L. I., & Kumashiro, K. K. (Eds.). (2014). *Diversifying the teacher workforce: Preparing and retaining highly effective teachers*. New York: Routledge.

Solorzano, D. G. (1997). Images and words that wound: Critical race theory, racial stereotyping, and teacher education. *Teacher Education Quarterly*, 5–19.

Solórzano, D. G. (2015). *Using the tools of Critical Race Theory and racial microaggressions to examine every day racism. [Powerpoint slides]*. Presented in Los Angeles, CA.

Solorzano, D., Allen, W. R., & Carroll, G. (2002). Keeping race in place: Racial microaggressions and campus racial climate at the University of California, Berkeley. *Chicano-Latino L. Rev.*, *23*, 15.

Solórzano, D. G., & Yosso, T. J. (2001). From racial stereotyping and deficit discourse toward a critical race theory in teacher education. *Multicultural Education, 9*(1), 2–8.

Solórzano, D. G., & Yosso, T. J. (2002). Critical race methodology: Counter-storytelling as an analytical framework for education research. *Qualitative inquiry*, *8*(1), 23–44.

Yosso, T. (2005). Whose culture has capital? A critical race theory discussion of community cultural wealth. *Race, Ethnicity and Education, 8*(1), 69–92.

Zeichner, K. M. (1993). Connecting genuine teacher development to the struggle for social justice. *Journal of Education for Teaching, 19*(1), 5–20.

Institute for Teachers of Color (ITOC) Committed to Racial Justice Commentary

ANA MARIA VILLEGAS

Contradictory trends in the racial/ethnic makeup of the U.S. student population and the teaching force in elementary and secondary schools, first noticed in the 1980s, focused the national spotlight on the shortage of teachers of color (Villegas, 1997). In 1972, the first year the U.S. Department of Education collected demographic data for the newly desegregated schools, students of color made up 22% of total enrollments and teachers of color accounted for 12% of the teaching force, a gap of 10 percentage points; by the mid 1980s, the disparity between the two groups had spiked to 17 percentage points, with students of color comprising 27% of total enrollments and teachers of color accounting for a mere 10% of the workforce (National Education Association [NEA], 2003; U.S. Department of Education, 2001). Alarmed by the conflicting demographics some scholars of color warned that without decisive intervention the widening racial/ethnic gap between students of color and their teachers would only grow in the years ahead (Cole, 1986; Graham, 1987; Irvine, 1988; Witty, 1986). In so doing, they helped to frame the shortage of teachers of color as a critical policy problem.

The overriding argument for diversifying the teaching force is that teachers of color are well positioned to promote the academic learning and overall life chances of students of color because they bring to the profession insight into these students' cultural backgrounds and everyday experiences (Milner, 2006; Villegas & Irvine, 2010). A central aspect of this argument is that compared to their white counterparts, people of color are more likely to enter teaching with the attitudes and dispositions needed to serve as agents of change in schools (Dingus, 2006; Fránquiz, Salazar, & DiNicolo, 2011; Kauchak & Burback, 2003; Rios & Montecinos, 1999; Su, 1997). This is because they know from first-hand experience what life is like for people of color in the United States. They are well aware that schools are not leveled playing fields on which all students prove their merit. That is, they understand that built into virtually every school and classroom are practices that place students of color at a decided disadvantage in the learning process, including unequal access to school resources, a non-inclusive curriculum, biased testing, and low teacher expectations, to mention just some (Kauchak & Burback, 2003; Rios & Montecinos, 1999; Su, 1997). If properly tapped by teacher educators and professional development facilitators, these experiences and insights—and the sociocultural consciousness they engender—could serve as a powerful resource for preparing teachers of color to engage in the reconstruction of schools to make them equitable for students who color. In fact, the addition of large numbers of teachers of color who are appropriately prepared with the knowledge and tools needed to act as agents of change and advocates for historically marginalized students represents our best chance to make schools more democratic and just.

Given the potential benefit of a diverse teaching force, it is encouraging to learn that the hard work of those who have fought for teacher diversity policies over the past 25 years or so has significantly expanded the number of teachers of color in elementary and secondary U.S. schools. To put this growth into perspective, in 1987—just a few years before states began adopting teacher diversity policies—public schools employed fewer than 300,000 teachers of color; by 2007 that number had risen to more than 575,000, a notable 92% growth over the 20-year period (Villegas, Strom, & Lucas, 2012). However, it would be unrealistic, if not unfair, to expect people of color to help narrow the entrenched racial/ethnic achievement gap without the benefit of professional growth experiences that enable them to use their unique cultural knowledge and perspectives in the service of students of color. To maximize the benefits that can be derived from a diverse teaching force requires educators to move beyond issues of recruitment and seriously attend to the preparation of teachers of color. Unfortunately, programs of preservice preparation and professional development have evaded their responsibility in this matter. In general, they give little or no attention to how to prepare teachers of color to use their insiders' experiences as members of communities of color to shape their pedagogy and define their roles as teachers (Cochran-Smith & Villegas, 2016; Montecinos, 2004; Sheets & Chew, 2002; Villegas & Davis, 2008). Left to figure this out on their own, it is not surprising that many teachers of color report feeling ill prepared to do the work that draws them to teaching—reconstructing schools for students of color (Villegas & Lucas, 2004). The sense of isolation, marginalization, and frustration resulting from such professional abandonment leave many teachers of color vulnerable to attrition (Parker & Hood, 1995).

The Institute for Teachers of Color (ITOC) Committed to Racial Justice (ITOC), which is featured in this volume, was purposefully designed to tackle this major gap in the preparation and development that teachers of color typically receive in traditional programs. A grassroots initiative, ITOC offers teachers of color professional preparation that builds on their strengths while addressing their needs, something neither university-based preservice programs nor programs of alternate routes to teaching are designed to do. As Pham and Kohli explained, "ITOC is intended as a community building, professional development space for teachers of Color to explore the racial climate of their schools, receive leadership training to navigate these realities, and strategize how to create racially transformative classrooms and schools." This mission helps explain the broad appeal ITOC has among teachers of color, mostly in the San Francisco Bay area where the program operates, but increasingly among educators from other parts of the country. As part of a three-day summer institute, the central component of ITOC, participants are introduced to critical race theory, the framework that lends conceptual coherence to the variety of learning opportunities to which participants are exposed. This well selected framework gives participating teachers of color a lens for analyzing racial issues in schools and understanding their underlying dynamics, the terminology for naming and discussing those issues, and tools for confronting the problems identified. During the three-day institute, participants are also carefully guided as they apply ideas learned to the development of action plans intended to systematically confront an issue of equity at play in their respective schools. Participants are encouraged to reach out to peers in their ITOC cohort for encouragement and support as they implement their action plans during the school year.

Beyond the critical race theory framework the program uses, which Pham and Kohli discussed in detail in their chapter, three other features of the ITOC professional development program merit attention. First, the criteria that program facilitators used to select participants enable ITOC to maximize its impact. As detailed by Pham and Kohli, to be considered for participation, applicants must demonstrate advanced racial literacy, a social justice orientation, leadership skills, and a willingness to use ideas learned to tackle issues of racism in their local school settings. By working with a group of teachers who are favorably predisposed to acting as critical educators and agents of change, program facilitators are able to create an intimate learning environment of like-minded teachers and cover extensive ground during the three-day summer institute, something not possible were they to be working with a less selective group of teachers. The intensity of the various professional learning opportunities offered during those three weeks helps explain the programs' profound influence on participating teachers' sense of agency to challenge the status quo, as the three case studies in the Pham and Kohli chapter illustrate. Equally important, because participants not only develop an action plan during the three-day institute but also commit to implementing those plans in their own schools during the school year that follows the training, the program has a much broader impact on schools, teachers, and students. The three case studies also give insight into the indirect impact of this well conceptualized critical professional development program.

Another salient feature of ITOC is the active engagement of participating teachers of color in their professional learning. Rather than passively transmitting ideas about critical race theory to the teachers, they are provided learning opportunities that actively involve them in discussing structural racism and liberatory pedagogy, reflecting on their personal experiences as people of color and role as critical teachers, identifying and analyzing issues of inequalities prevalent in their schools, and developing a systematic plan of action to address those concerns, among other activities. Professional learning opportunities of this nature reflect the sociocultural perspective on teacher learning that informs ITOC and are in keeping with effective professional practices documented in the professional development research literature (Desimone, Porter, Garet, Yoon, & Birman, 2002).

The third notable feature of the professional development offered through ITOC I highlight here is the program's focus on collaboration and community. While collaboration among teachers in professional development contexts has been found highly effective in affecting changes in teacher practices and in improving student achievement (Wayne, Yoon, Zhu, Cronen, & Garet, 2008), collaboration is conceivably an even more powerful factor in promoting professional learning for teachers of color, many of whom report experiencing a deep sense of isolation, marginalization, and alienation in programs of pre-professional preparation (Amos, 2013; Chung & Harrison, 2015; Irizarry, 2011) and in the schools where they teach (Phillips & Nava, 2011). Thus, immersion in a supportive professional learning community comprised exclusively of teachers of color who share a commitment to social justice, and where participants are able to openly discuss issues of racial injustice—the type of community ITOC creates—gives participating teachers of color a healing and validating experience, one that frames their difference from mainstream cultural groups as an asset, countering the deficit-oriented messages they often receive in traditional preparation programs (Haddix, 2010; Irizarry, 2011; Kohli, 2014). As Pham and Kohli explained, to build a strong sense of community ITOC facilitators purposefully use team-building exercises and frequently place participants to work in groups, thereby building collaborative relationships among them and ultimately helping them to see themselves as part of a broader community of change agents.

Without question, ITOC is a unique professional development program for teachers of color. As detailed in the Pham and Kohli chapter and discussed in this commentary, the program uses critical race theory as a unifying framework for its teacher learning curriculum, selects teachers of color for participation based on well thought out criteria, actively engages participants in their professional learning, and builds a collaborative learning community that affirms and validates the experiences of teachers of color. Clearly, traditional programs of pre-professional preparation and ongoing professional development—whether based at universities or associated with alternate routes to teaching—have much to learn from ITOC about how to create organizational and curricular spaces that acknowledge and capitalize on the experiences teachers of color bring to teaching while simultaneously addressing their specific needs. To this end, investing resources to more carefully document the implementation of ITOC, more rigorously assess the program's impact on participants and beyond, and more widely disseminate results could contribute in significant ways to ultimately realizing the promise of a diverse teaching force.

REFERENCES

Amos, Y. T. (2013). Becoming a teacher of color: Mexican bilingual paraprofessionals' journey to teach. *Teacher Education Quarterly, 40*(3), 51–73.

Chung, J. Y., & Harrison, L. M. (2015). Toward an ethnic studies critique for teacher education. *Multicultural Perspectives, 17*(1), 4–12. doi: 10.1080/15210960.2014.984719

Cochran-Smith, M., & Villegas, A. M. (with Abrams, L., Chavez-Moreno, L., Mills, T., & Stern, R.) (2016). Research on teacher preparation: Charting the landscape of a sprawling field. In D. Gitomer & Courtney A. Bell (Eds.), *Handbook of research on teaching* (5th ed.). New York, NY: Routledge/AERA.

Cole, B. P. (1986). The black educator: An endangered species. *Journal of Negro Education, 55*(3), 326–334. doi.org/10.2307/2295103

Desimone, L. M., Porter, A. C., Garet, M. S., Yoon, K. S., & Birman, B. F. (2002). Effects of professional development on teachers' instruction: Results from a three-year longitudinal study. *Educational Evaluation and Policy Analysis, 24*, 81–112.

Dingus, J. (2006). "Doing the best we could": African American teachers' counterstories on school desegregation. *The Urban Review, 38*(3), 211–233.

Fránquiz, M. E., Salazar, M. d. C., & DeNicolo, C. P. (2011). Challenging majoritarian tales: Portraits of bilingual teachers deconstructing deficit views of bilingual learners. *Bilingual Research Journal, 34*(3), 279–300. doi.org/10.1080/15235882.2011.625884

Graham, P. A. (1987). Black teachers: A drastically scarce resource. *Phi Delta Kappan, 68*(8), 598–605.

Haddix, M. (2010). No longer on the margins: Researching the hybrid literate identities of Black and Latina preservice teachers. *Research in the Teaching of English, 45*(2), 97–123.

Irizarry, J. G. (2011). En la lucha: The struggles and triumphs of Latino/a preservice teachers. *Teachers College Record, 113*(12), 2804–2835.

Irvine, J. J. (1988). An analysis of the problem of the disappearing Black educator. *Elementary School Journal, 88*(5), 503–514.

Kauchak, D., & Burback, M. D. (2003). Voices in the classroom: Case studies of minority teacher candidates. *Action in Teacher Education*, 25(1), 63–75.

Kohli, R. (2014). Unpacking internalized racism: Teachers of color striving for racially just classrooms. *Race Ethnicity and Education, 17*(3), 367–387.

Milner, H. R. (2006). The promise of Black teachers' success with Black students. *Educational Foundations, 20*(2–3), 89–104.

Montecinos, C. (2004). Paradoxes in multicultural teacher education research: Students of color positioned as objects while ignored as subjects. *International Journal of Qualitative Studies in Education, 17*(2), 167–181. doi.org/10.1080/09518390310001653853

National Education Association. (2003). *Status of the American Public School Teacher.* Washington, DC: National Education Association.

Parker, L., & Hood, S. (1995). Minority students vs. majority faculty and administrators in teacher education: Perspectives on the clash of cultures. *The Urban Review, 27*(2), 159–174.

Phillips, D. K., & Nava, R. C. (2011). Biopower, disciplinary power, and the production of the "good Latino/a teacher". *Discourse: Studies in the Cultural Politics of Education, 32*(1), 71–83.

Rios, F., & Montecinos, C. (1999). Advocating social justice and cultural affirmation: Ethnically diverse preservice teachers' perspectives on multicultural education. *Equity & Excellence in Education, 32*(3), 66–76. doi.org/10.1080/1066568990320308

Sheets, R. H., & Chew, L. (2002). Absent from the research, present in our classrooms: Preparing culturally responsive Chinese American teachers. *Journal of Teacher Education, 53*(2), 127–141. doi.org/10.1177/0022487102053002005

Su, Z. (1997). Teaching as a profession and as a career: Minority candidates' perspectives. *Teaching and Teacher Education, 13*(3), 325–340.

U.S. Department of Education. (2001). *Bureau of the Census, October current population surveys, 1972–2000.* Table 3–1 Percentage distribution of public school students enrolled in grades K-12 who were minorities. Retrieved from http://nces.ed.gov/programs/coe/2002/section1/tables/t03_1.asp

Villegas, A. M. (1997). Increasing the racial and ethnic diversity of the U.S. teaching force. In B. J. Biddle, T. L. Good, & I. F. Goodson (Eds.), *International handbook of teachers and teaching* (Vol. 3, pp. 267–301). Netherlands: Springer.

Villegas, A. M., & Davis, D. (2008). Preparing teachers of color to confront racial/ethnic disparities in educational outcomes. In M. Cochran-Smith, S. Feiman-Nemser, & J. McIntyre (Eds.), *Handbook of research in teacher education: Enduring issues in changing contexts* (pp. 583–605, 3rd ed.). Mahwah, NJ: Lawrence Erlbaum.

Villegas, A. M., & Irvine, J. (2010). Diversifying the teaching force: An examination of major arguments. *Urban Review, 42*(3), 175–192. doi: 10.1007/s11256-010-0150-1

Villegas, A. M., & Lucas, T. F. (2004). Diversifying the teacher workforce: A retrospective and prospective analysis. In M. Smylie & D. Miretzky (Eds.), *Developing the teacher workforce: The 103rd yearbook of the National Society for the Study of Education* (Vol. 103, pp. 70–104). Chicago: University of Chicago Press.

Villegas, A. M., Strom, K., & Lucas, T. (2012). Closing the racial/ethnic gap between students of color and their teachers: An elusive goal. *Equity & Excellence in Education, 45*(2), 283–301.

Wayne, A. J., Yoon, K. S., Zhu, P., Cronen, S., & Garet, M. S. (2008). Experimenting with teacher professional development: Motives and methods. *Educational Researcher, 37*(8), 469–479.

Witty, E. P. (1986). Testing teacher performance. *Journal of Negro Education, 55*(3), 267–279.

CHAPTER SIX

Reimagining Teacher Development

CONRA D. GIST

In this volume I have been concerned with programs and initiatives that have critical teaching and learning orientations in order to (a) identify structures that define them, (b) focus the goals of teacher development on cultivating critically conscious Teachers of Color, and (c) consider implications for ARTs committed to justice, communities, and visionaries. Specifically, I wanted to grapple with the central question: *how can ARTs be framed, developed, and executed from critical perspectives that work to challenge and dismantle systems of oppression for Teachers of Color*? The program portraits and accompanying commentary by senior scholars in the field begin to provide potential answers to this question. In different ways, each program reveals the possible seeds of critical teacher development for Teachers of Color. To better understand how these structures are built and take shape, in the following section, I use the four attributes of critical development for Teachers of Color to identify common themes across the program initiatives.

CRITICAL TEACHER DEVELOPMENT FOR TEACHERS OF COLOR: A CROSS-ANALYSIS OF PROGRAMS

A central premise of this collection is that programs guided by critical teacher development for Teachers of Color should encompass some combination of the following attributes:

1. Develop anti-racist educational structures that support the recruitment and retention of Teachers of Color
2. Create and employ responsive and tailored preparation practices that address the philosophical and praxis teaching and learning needs and strengths of Teachers of Color
3. Provide advocacy, organizing, and justice vehicles for Teachers of Color to identify, challenge, and restructure power relations and social inequality in schools and neighborhood communities
4. View and position local community partnerships and leadership as integral and vital to the program mission, impact and long-term sustainability

In the critical teacher development framework, anti-racist educational structures that support the recruitment and retention of Teachers of Color are identified by the implementation of policies and practices (e.g., targeted program mission and selection criteria focused on strengths of Teachers of Color, cohort groups, mentorship, financial and academic supports) that work to dismantle interlocking structural barriers (e.g., poor K-12 schooling experiences, unqualified/unresponsive teachers, meager socioeconomic opportunities, deficit curriculum, institutionalized racism in policies and practices, dissonance between home and school cultures) that can prevent access to teacher education programs and restrict their ability to navigate the system to become teachers of record and remain in K-12 classrooms. Key to this attribute is not simply an acknowledgement of issues confronting Teachers of Color, but the strategic creation of structures that disrupt racist patterns of limited entry into, and retainment within, the teaching profession. Implementing assessment protocols to investigate and address program strengths and weaknesses, and engage in the process of constant iterative refinement, is also important for sustaining anti-racist educational structures to enhance the teaching and learning experiences of Teachers of Color (Gist, 2014a). The second attribute, tailored and responsive preparation, is understood as critical pedagogies, curriculum, and instructional practices (e.g., attention to critical and culturally sustaining pedagogies, critical race theory, valuing of the community teacher and local funds of knowledge, community organizing, and advancing social justice) in the context of coursework, fieldwork, and teaching experiences that are focused on supporting and developing Teachers of Color to be critically conscious and positively impactful educators for students, schools, and communities. The role of critically conscious and culturally responsive teacher educators (i.e., those committed to challenging hierarchies of power and privilege that limit the academic and professional achievement of Teachers of Color frequently marginalized in teacher education programs) is essential to this process (Gist, 2014b, 2016).

The third attribute, vehicles for Teachers of Color to challenge social inequality, is viewed as access to intentional and focused mechanisms or entities (e.g., Teachers of Color advocacy/inquiry groups, organizing campaigns, neighborhood block meetings) that cultivate and build on community solidarity and advocate for social justice commitments (e.g., petition for equitable funding, lobby legislatures for fair testing evaluations, fundraising for starting local community based organization or business). The idea of "vehicles" is connected to the notion that it is not enough to discuss unjust power relations and social inequality without providing the means to mobilize (e.g., framing narratives, accessing and partnering with indigenous groups, integrating multiple standpoints; Franklin, 2014), and act. Finally, programs that value, recognize, and integrate community-based partnerships (e.g., neighborhood associations, non-profit organizations, community centers, local businesses and clubs) and leadership (e.g., local government officials, school principals, youth and community organizers and activists, parents) with respect to teaching and learning along the teacher development continuum (i.e., recruitment, preparation, induction, and retention) evidence the last attribute of critical teacher development for Teachers of Color. For this attribute, the program moves from being an island unto itself to seeing its mission and work as intimately tied to commitments and efforts of local community organizations and leaders, and thus, seeks their direction and input at each stage of the teacher development continuum.

Collectively these four attributes point to structures, vehicles, dispositions, knowledges, and practices that strategically support the recruitment and retention of Teachers of Color. Although I explain each attribute separately, and there are overlaps between them, the individual description of attributes assists with making sense and organizing our efforts to enact thoughtful and focused interventions to increase the racial/ethnic diversity of our teacher workforce. To varying degrees, these attributes of critical teacher development for Teachers of Color are evident across the different ART and professional development program portraits. In order to examine and explicate key themes across the programs, the following section will describe evidence related to each critical teacher development attribute and contemplate the ways in which the programs do and do not work to dismantle systems of oppression for Teachers of Color. Table 6.1 outlines connections between dimensions of critical teacher development for Teachers of Color and each program (i.e., Teach Tomorrow in Oakland (TTO); Grow Your

Own Illinois (GYO-IL); California Mini-Corps (CMC); Institute for Teachers of Color (ITOC) Committed to Racial Justice.

Table 6.1. Cross-Analysis of Programs Applying Critical Teacher Development Framework.

Critical Teacher Development Attributes	ART and Professional Development Initiatives for TOCs
Anti-racist educational structures: the implementation of policies and practices that work to dismantle racist barriers that prevent access to teacher education programs and restrict their ability to navigate through programs to become teachers of record and remain in K-12 classrooms	TTO o Program designed to recruit Teachers of Color and disrupt the outsourcing of teachers from national recruitment agencies o A community based and responsive selection criteria for program entry o Rigorous and critical selection of TTO teacher leaders/coaches o Built in career ladder opportunities to work toward Masters degree and receive additional pay (financial supports) o Individual support plans for TTO teachers
	GYO-IL o The provision of financial supports for books, university fees, tutoring, childcare, transportation, stipends during student teaching o Cohort meetings to discuss academic and emotional issues o Recruitment framework and selection criteria requires participants be a parent, paraeducator, community leader, or an individual from a community with a hard to staff school o Provision of community and higher education coordinators to offer supports
	CMC o Prioritizes and values candidates from migrant backgrounds and communities o Inclusion of college coordinator in program funding o Teachers organized in cohorts as a type of affinity grouping o Strategic placement in migrant communities early and often o Mentorship for the duration of the program (e.g., assistance with college prep, course selection, monitoring grades, prep for teacher certification exams, portfolio management, guidance on how to develop effective relationships)

Critical Teacher Development Attributes	ART and Professional Development Initiatives for TOCs
	ITOC o Creation of intentional cohorts of TOCs to address race and racism in ways that can support retention once they enter schools o Naming and valuing racial literacy expertise in the selection of Teachers of Color for the Institute
Tailored and responsive preparation: critical pedagogies, curriculum, and instructional practices in the context of coursework, fieldwork, and teaching experiences focused on supporting and developing Teachers of Color to be critically conscious and positively impactful for students, schools, and communities	**TTO** o Place-based education theory drives preparation model o "Reach and teach" philosophy o "Tune-up Tuesdays" that provide instructional enhancement opportunities o Instructional coaches and university work together to ensure responsive curricular alignment between university-based theory and classroom-based practice o Teacher leaders are well-versed in anti-racist pedagogy and can model teaching excellence in local community schools
	GYO-IL o Curriculum driven and informed by issues on the ground related to social, economic, and racial justice o CBOs provide leadership development training and exploration of social justice issues impacting their communities o Close articulation between teacher education and CBOs to ensure adequate teaching placements and resources to successfully complete coursework o Teacher education program adapts curriculum based on engagement with and lessons learned from community based organizations
	CMC o Cognitive coaching from college coordinator o Offers monthly professional development sessions to support tutor effectiveness o Bi-monthly observations and feedback from master teachers o Summer orientation and training for different placement assignments

Critical Teacher Development Attributes	ART and Professional Development Initiatives for TOCs
	ITOC o Explore racial climate at school, receive leadership training and strategize how to create racially transformative schools o Exposure to critical frameworks and other fields of study (i.e., ethnic studies, psychology, women and gender studies, social work and community organizing) o Employ a model of critical professional development (i.e., community building, systemic plan for racial justice work, cohort of racial justice minded peers, theory driven content facilitated by people of color, and reflection, healing and self-care) o Engage in asset framing of communities of color
Vehicles for justice: access to intentional and focused mechanisms or entities that cultivate and build on community solidarity and advocate for social justice commitments	**TTO** o The creation of TTO Teacher Leaders model to facilitate PDs that have a socially conscious mindset and support leadership development for various school and community roles o Men in the Classroom initiative that creates a safe place to share strategies for survival and works against the revolving door phenomenon
	GYO-IL o Community organizing opportunities with local community based organizations for teachers and candidates o Opportunities to join legislative campaigns to advocate for funding o Offer legislative training sessions to help prepare teachers and candidates to speak to legislators o Cohort groups are created based on neighborhoods and geography o At cohort meetings, teachers and teacher candidates discuss issues like the foreclosure crisis, lack of affordable housing, school to prison pipeline, mental health clinics, gun violence and how to organize and partner with other CBOs and community leaders to address these issues o Developed and organized coalition to change teacher testing policies at the state level

Critical Teacher Development Attributes	ART and Professional Development Initiatives for TOCs
	CMC o CMC summer orientation and training program brings migrant tutors together in solidarity to serve migrant communities and gain self-efficacy to tackle the educational challenges they face
	ITOC o Encourage institute participants to create critical inquiry groups in their own school buildings and local communities o Create spaces for healing and honoring the voices of TOCs—in these spaces participants gain self-efficacy and strength to move forward
Partnership and leadership: value, recognize, and integrate community-based partnerships and leadership along the teacher development continuum	**TTO** o Work with local faith-based agencies and community organizations in the recruitment process o Rely on partnerships with teacher education programs, and school/community leaders for selection and support of teachers o Utilize community partnerships to offer fieldwork opportunities and supports
	CMC o Function as a state alliance with community partnerships with colleges and regional migrant educational programs o Develop local school partnerships in migrant communities to establish internship programs
	GYO-IL o The program is a partnership of community based organizations, institutions of higher education, and public school districts (as specified by GYO Teacher Education Act) designed to identify and support local community leadership o Selection interviews typically incorporate a group of higher education, community based organization, and school district partners
	ITOC o Partnerships are primarily with other university programs (i.e., ethnic studies and women) and teacher leader social justice organizations (e.g., Free Minds Free People, NYCORE, and Teachers 4 Social Justice) committed to TOCs o Recruiting community based TOCs to prepare as leaders to challenge structures of racism at their school sites

ANTI-RACIST EDUCATIONAL STRUCTURES

Mission and Selection Criteria

Looking across the program initiatives, several themes are apparent with respect to anti-racist educational structures that work to dismantle barriers that prevent access to, and matriculation through, teacher education programs to become successful teachers of record. For one, the ART policies and practices are anchored in program missions and selection criteria committed to creating spaces in the educational field for Teachers of Color that did not previously exist. For example, the TTO program developed a selection model that incorporates valuing the strengths Teachers of Color can bring to the classroom (e.g., experiences within and commitments to community, connection with local community leaders, or cultural affinity connections with local school community). In other words, instead of noting these strengths as additional points of consideration at the bottom of the selection criteria, they are central to TTO's selection process. The selection of these future teachers is anchored in valuing the communities the teachers come from and will serve by seeking community leaders with educational commitments in their local neighborhoods. Hence, the selection criteria functions as an anti-racist educational tool by challenging protocols that delegitimize community cultural knowledge as valuable, which can work to restrict Teachers' of Color professional opportunities by devaluing strengths they may bring to the profession.

Similarly, the GYO-IL program incorporates a recruitment model that begins in the community first by looking to community based organizations and advocacy leaders to identify potential future teachers. There is a specific focus on community Teachers of Color who might otherwise be overlooked because they do not have college degrees, are older, or have professional experiences that are associated with lower class workers (e.g., crossing guards, store clerks, bus drivers, janitors). The GYO-IL mission (i.e., recruiting and retaining local community Teachers of Color) is integrated with selection criteria that prioritize candidates being from and having long-term commitments to the community. The ITOC initiative also has specific selection criteria that prioritizes Teachers of Color with racial literacy knowledge and commitments to work toward racial justice in their schools. Again, there is a clear link between the ITOC mission (i.e., supporting racial justice Teachers of Color) and selection decisions to admit Teachers of Color who exhibit racial literacy knowledge and commitments to racial justice. A key takeaway across the programs is that the mission to recruit and support Teachers of Color is yoked with selection criteria that recognizes and values their strengths and justice commitments, thereby providing initial access to the teaching profession (or in the case of ITOC, access to critical professional development). This anti-racist educational practice challenges selection models that normalize the deprioritization of community expertise and knowledges as a significant indicator of future teacher capacity to thrive in local community schools.

A Range of Support

Once accepted in these programs, establishing certain policies and practices to address barriers that could limit the successful navigation of Teachers of Color in university settings requires a range of support. For the ARTs, these practices included the provision of financial, academic and mentorship supports. This was clearly apparent in the TTO, GYO-IL and CMC programs. The GYO-IL program provided a range of financial supports (i.e., college fees, books tutoring, childcare, transportation, stipends during student teaching), all of which are critical for the teacher population they serve. TTO noted creating career ladder opportunities as a type of financial support that can enable teachers to acquire additional monies while they are working to obtain teaching licenses. Also, CMC noted a broad range of mentorship supports, which included assistance with college prep, course selection, monitoring grades, prep for teacher certification exams, portfolio management, and guidance on how to develop effective relationships. The organizing and grouping of Teachers of Color in different types of cohorts was also noted as an anti-racist structural support. For example, in the case of GYO-IL, CMC and ITOC program initiatives, the cohort model was utilized as a tool to share academic resources, offer emotional supports, and/or create affinity groups to cultivate community among Teachers of Color to reduce struggles such as racial isolation, lack of resources, and misinformation about program procedures and requirements. Without such supports in place Teachers of Color can face an increased and disproportional likelihood to leave the profession before graduating (Lau, Dandy, & Hoffman, 2007).

Funding Program Leadership

The presence of program coordinators assigned in CMC, GYO-IL and TTO to guide Teachers of Color toward the successful completion of the program was also an important structure in the ARTs. For instance, GYO-IL utilized higher education and community based coordinators to facilitate and lead cohort meetings, offer professional development, and schedule individual checkpoints with Teachers of Color. TTO employed teacher leaders to offer the types of supports TTO teachers needed, were not receiving, but were critical to their ability to remain in the profession. Additionally, CMC created funding lines for college coordinators to offer significant mentorship opportunities. This might seem a small point for programs that consistently have stable funding lines, but when initiatives focused on Teachers of Color are not valued via an investment of financial capital, they can be heavily reliant on volunteers or some combination of part-time responsibilities on the part of different individuals. This often results in a lack of centralized leadership and consistent direction, which limits the ability of the program to execute, with integrity, anti-racist educational practices and policies for Teachers of Color. Thus, the allocation of funding for program coordinators to address barriers that problematize the successful program completion of Teachers of Color is key.

TAILORED AND RESPONSIVE PREPARATION

Teacher Learners

Making efforts to employ tailored and responsive teaching and learning experiences for teacher candidates and teachers may appear at first glance to be a commonsensical approach for any teacher education program worth its salt, but when you consider the implications for Teachers and Teacher Candidates of Color in particular, these commitments take on a different emphasis. For instance, TTO argues that the program is designed to create an anti-racist ART in order to disrupt a teaching reservation system that is overwhelming white (Sleeter, 2001). In this case, the underlying argument is traditional teacher education programs are typically designed for white middle class women (Chapman, 2011). The logical rationale, then, is that explicit efforts must be made to ensure ART programs are also driven by the needs of Teachers of Color. Teachers of Color who are older, working full-time jobs, and have additional community and familial commitments (such as the case with GYO-IL teachers) require a different structure and model. CMC students who come from migrant communities, which have a wealth of community cultural resources, but at the same time might not have college-readiness and academic preparedness to thrive in higher education, need tailored supports (Shroyer, Yahnke, Morales, Dunn, Lohfink, & Espinoza, 2009). And in the case of ITOC, recognizing the unmet needs and challenges Teachers of Color face when they leave teacher education programs, is precisely why the critical professional development model was created. In short, seeing who the teacher learners are (at the intersection of their racial, cultural, linguistic, familial, gendered, and classed socialized beings) in the program is necessary to ensure content and pedagogy is responsive to their needs and strengths.

Content and Pedagogy

Several different content topics, philosophies and pedagogies framed the teacher preparation and development curriculum offered to Teachers of Color by ARTs. For the CMC, the content and pedagogy focused on traditional topics (e.g., lesson planning, classroom management, and instructional strategies in math, English language arts and language development) and offered extensive practical learning preparation supports via bi-monthly observations and feedback, and cognitive coaching. Still, the strategic placement of teachers in migrant communities each summer for fieldwork experiences, coupled with the assignment of local tutoring commitments during the academic year, are signature components of the preparation model. Through their tutoring, student teaching, and fieldwork experiences, CMC teachers noted seeing their family and community members in the lives of students they tutor and teach. In this sense, the program design works to integrate CMC candidates' community connections in pedagogy and practice through consistent placement and service to migrant communities throughout their undergraduate experiences.

TTO and GYO-IL offered preparation that covered traditional topics, too, but their content and pedagogy also differed in noticeable ways. TTO had a "reach and teach" and place based education approach that was grounded in community commitments and cultural connections with students. The GYO-IL curriculum was driven by community issues on the ground related to economic, social, and racial justice, and teachers used the community issues and struggles to inform what they taught. Also, the community based organizations, in their cohort meetings, offered leadership training and pushed teachers to explore social justice issues. ITOC had the most explicit and detailed explanation of critically focused content and pedagogy, in part as a response to what was not being offered in traditional teacher education programs, and also to address the need to provide Teachers of Color with possible tools to remain and thrive in schools. The ITOC critical professional development model (i.e., an incorporation of community building, systemic plan for racial justice work, cohort of racial justice minded peers, theory driven content facilitated by people of color, and reflection, healing and self-care) centers race and racism in the teaching and learning experiences of Teachers of Color and provides possible pathways to transgress and address racial injustice in their schools and communities. There was also an intentional focus in ITOC on asset framing of Teachers and Communities of Color from a strength-based perspective.

Teacher Educators

Looking across the program initiatives, aside from university teacher education faculty, the people who are teaching and leading the preparation and development of Teachers of Color are varied, and inclusive of community based organization leaders and organizers, faculty from disciplinary backgrounds outside the education field, and teacher leaders from the school district. This reflects an expansive, rather than limited, vision of who should play a role in shaping the teaching and learning experiences of Teachers of Color. The possible benefits of the incorporation of multiple stakeholders in the learning process are that these relationships work (potentially) toward a more integrated system of content and practice opportunities for Teachers of Color and emphasize learning in praxis. For example, TTO noted the need to bridge the gap between university and school district approaches and methodologies in order for Teachers of Color to be better equipped to meet the day-to-day challenges of teaching in the classroom. Recognizing this as an issue early in the program's inception, the GYO-IL program worked to establish close articulation between community based organizations and teacher education programs to ensure Teachers of Color are being responsively and effectively prepared.

There also appears to be an explicit focus on involving People of Color, in general, to lead as teacher educators, or at the very least, people who have deep-seated critical commitments to local community schools and Teachers of Color. ITOC emphasized the importance of having content facilitated by community leaders and teacher educators of Color to have people who reflect the positionality of Teachers of Color and may be more knowledgeable of the types of challenges they face. For similar reasons that Teachers of Color are seen as assets in K-12 settings (e.g., higher expectations, cultural bridge builders, role models and justice commitments), the same holds true for higher education and professional learning environments (Gist, 2014a). TTO echoed this perspective as well when the program realized content and pedagogy needed to be facilitated by someone able to foster a learning context that allowed critical and difficult dialogues to take place, which often means involving Teachers of Color to lead as facilitators.

VEHICLES FOR JUSTICE

Providing Teachers of Color access to vehicles for justice was noticeable in different ways across the ARTs. These mechanisms and entities were linchpins to realizing the aims of the critical tailored and responsive preparation Teachers of Color received in order to be effective in their schools and communities. In the ARTs, the creation of spaces for Teachers of Color, coalitions and campaigns, and inquiry action groups, were vehicles employed by the programs to cultivate community solidarity and advocate for justice.

Spaces for Teachers of Color

Through various types of training, the programs took up conscious-raising activities to mobilize Teachers of Color in solidarity and advocate their social justice commitments. For example, TTO, recognizing the inadequate district professional development being offered Teachers of Color, created a Teacher Leader pipeline that positioned TTO graduates and successful community teachers to lead socially conscious trainings to address real challenges TTO teachers face in schools and communities. These trainings functioned as a vehicle for justice because they created space for solidarity that previously did not exist for Teachers of Color and better equipped them to realize their social justice commitments in their classrooms. In particular, the TTO Men in the Classroom series attends to the intersection of gender and race among Teachers of Color, recognizing the need for a specific structure to combat small numbers and honor the distinct experiences they face. As a potential mobilizing space, the Men of Color are able to address obstacles that may be frustrating their social justice commitments in the classroom and identify possible solutions. ITOC, through a 3-day professional development institute, worked to, among other things, create spaces for healing and honoring Teachers' of Color voices that did not previously exist. Recognizing the challenges of racial isolation, coupled with the high turnover of Teachers of Color taking place in comparison to their white counterparts, ITOC created spaces that allow for healing, reflecting, and self-care to take place.

GYO-IL also offered a space for Teachers of Color that was not just focused on advocating for educational justice, but conscious-raising related to broader forces of structural racism and social inequality in local school communities (e.g., the foreclosure crisis, need for mental health clinics, gun violence) that directly impact the lives of students and families. It was a space to raise awareness and make sense of how they can be at times stymied by interlocking structures of oppression. Collectively, these spaces functioned as both a shield from forces of oppression and fertile ground to develop plans for action.

Coalitions and Campaigns

Many of the social justice efforts that take place in conscious-raising trainings focus on learning about individual efforts Teachers of Color can take up in their classrooms (Banks & Banks, 2013). This is positive and valuable because it pierces through a type of apathy and powerlessness that can characterize the justice workers role in the classroom. Still, collective efforts to work on the side of justice outside the individual classroom can be equally beneficial. GYO-IL illustrated what this work can look like most profoundly because the genesis of the program was launched in Chicago by organizing school communities and building coalitions among community organizations committed to advocating for local community teachers. This laborious community organizing effort eventually resulted in the GYO Teacher Act, which created GYO-IL programs across the state. It is worth noting that TTO started in response to local community turmoil, too, which prompted the mayor to designate a community based taskforce to determine how to best meet the needs of Oakland's children; this district level organizing resulted in the creation of TTO. But the coalition work of GYO-IL, for example, extended beyond the initial creation of the program to also include participation in additional citywide coalitions (e.g., working with community based organizations to pressure legislatures to address testing bias among Teachers of Color, which resulted in designating an alternative test measure to demonstrate competency).

GYO-IL also led yearly campaigns to lobby state legislatures for additional funding allocations to support the sustainability of the program. In order to engage GYO-IL teachers in these campaigns, GYO-IL provided trainings through local community organizations in their networks on how to talk to legislatures about GYO. Whether participating in a cross-organizational coalition committed to addressing an educational issue, or working on local campaigns within the GYO-IL organization, Teachers of Color were part of a collective to advocate for social justice that moved them beyond individual justice work in the classroom to address broader social justice issues.

Inquiry Action Groups

Whereas mobilizing groups within and across organizations to advance social justice efforts represented a broad collective approach, there were also justice vehicles developed in the form of inquiry action groups by the ART and professional development initiatives. For instance, ITOC, as a professional development initiative, prepared Teachers of Color in their institutes to develop a systemic plan for racial justice work, that at times included building a cohort of racial justice minded peers in their local schools and communities. The intention here is that learning about such groups equip and prepare Teachers of Color to create, organize and lead conscious-raising, healing and voice-centering spaces that have the potential for community mobilization. The ITOC teachers spotlighted in the program portrait are examples of how Teachers of Color who engage in the institute eventually worked to cultivate inquiry action spaces in their schools to research and address racial justice issues in their school and local communities. In other words, across varying schools and community contexts, inquiry action groups were being utilized by ITOC Teachers of Color as vehicles to organize and create actions for racial justice. GYO-IL also worked to offer professional development on inquiry action groups as a mechanism by which Teachers of Color can learn to take the lead, confront justice issues, and consider and plan concrete actions they might take.

PARTNERSHIP AND LEADERSHIP

The valuing, recognition, and integration of community based partnerships and leadership along the teacher development continuum took place in various ways across the ARTs via centering community voices, establishing organizational partnerships, and reimagining leadership. The gist of this critical teacher development attribute is partnership with community, not as an afterthought but at the forefront, and leadership that embodies the valuing of local community knowledges and perspectives.

Community Voices

The centering of community voices in the selection process for Teachers of Color was a salient practice among the ARTs, particularly in the case of TTO and GYO-IL programs. TTO first involved community perspectives by reaching out to faith-based organizations, non-profits, and other groups who work with and reach local community members. TTO also asks candidates to teach lessons in current TTO members classrooms and local Boys and Girls clubs to ensure the spaces they work to demonstrate teaching prowess are not in artificial sites, but real and authentic community spaces. Further, community members, students, principals, and current TTO teachers observe the teaching sample and use a rubric to indicate whether they would be good teachers in Oakland's educational community. In this sense, there are multiple community stakeholders involved in this selection process that determines whether or not the teachers are hired. Also, the focus of hiring power shifts from solely valuing school district leaders' views of teacher quality, to "centering student and community voices" to own the process. In a different way, community voices are also instrumental in the selection process of GYO-IL. The primary process for identifying potential Teachers of Color starts in local school communities with community based organizations identifying community leaders who have a passion for the community and education. Instead of the teacher education program being the primary selector for potential teachers, the community initiates the process. And before candidates can gain entry in these programs, they must first go through an interview protocol that involves multiple stakeholders early in the process (e.g., school district, community based organization, higher education partners). In this sense, the community and a coalition of stakeholders are active early in the selection of GYO-IL candidates.

Organizational Partnerships

For all the ART and professional development initiatives, partnerships were vital for the execution of programs. In terms of the overall organizational structure, CMC and GYO-IL are reliant on statewide networks. CMC has a statewide network of 22 community colleges and state universities and 20 migrant educational regional offices that provide educational access and opportunity for migrant communities in school districts across the state. CMC also worked to establish strong relationships with school districts in migrant communities for summer internships. The original bill that chartered the creation of the Grow Your Own Teacher Act requires that programs are organized in a consortium (i.e., a collective of a community based organization, institution of higher education, and a school district), and these consortia are organized throughout the state of Illinois to recruit and retain Teachers of Color. ITOC, as a professional development initiative, noted organizational connections with other social justice organizations being important, for the initial creation of the institute as well as establishing recruitment base to solicit participation of racial justice minded Teachers of Color.

The quality of ARTs partnerships with institutions of higher education appeared to be particularly important during the preparation phase. TTO noted challenges that can arise when productive partnerships are not in place (e.g., course timing and location, assignment of fieldwork placement, financial costs), and how they can be prohibitive for Teachers of Color seeking to enter the profession. And when funding did in fact become an obstacle for TTO, they partnered with community based organizations to create alternative arrangements for student teaching and fieldwork hours. GYO-IL, on the other hand, reflected a more integrated partnership with institutions of higher education that facilitated provisions and supports for the successful matriculation of GYO-IL students through the program. These types of organizational connections matter in terms of ensuring the provision of tailored and responsive preparation that equips Teachers of Color to be effective when they become teachers of record in classrooms.

Reimagining Leadership

A focus on local and community based leadership is addressed in some combination of the program mission, preparation, and organizational structure of all the ARTs. For one, the efforts of the ARTs are focused on reimagining educational leaders as people who come from the local community. ITOC is creating a pipeline for racially conscious Teachers of Color to become justice leaders in their schools and communities. Many of these participants are racially isolated and without a community of like-minded peers; therefore, they are being prepared and challenged to become leaders who can create spaces for Teachers of Color that do not yet exist in school and local communities. Their plights of struggle as lone justice warriors are being reimagined as potential mobilizing sites to organize a community of racial justice advocates. TTO, noting an absence of professional development leaders who were responsive to the needs of Teachers of Color, created a leadership pipeline for TTO teachers in the local Oakland community to lead and reimagine anti-racist pedagogy in schools. Again, noticing a vacuum of racially conscious professional development leadership, TTO recruited Teachers of Color to fill the void and be the teacher leaders they wanted to see in professional development sessions. The CMC program challenges the deficit narrative of needing to help and save migrant communities, by reframing them as sources of untapped leadership and challenging migrant community members to become teachers and educational leaders. GYO-IL reimagines leadership from a grassroots perspective by recruiting local leaders within the community, opposed to outside the community, to be architects of change. Collectively, leadership is reimagined and developed across the ART and professional development initiatives in terms of who is being recruited to the profession as future educational leaders, and the positioning of Teachers of Color to lead community organizing and professional development opportunities.

IMPLICATIONS FOR ARTs IN THEORY, RESEARCH, POLICY, AND PRAXIS

The idea of framing ARTs from critical perspectives that can work to challenge and dismantle systems of oppression for Teachers of Color can be puzzling, to say the least, given research and analysis highlighting the challenges they typically present: contributing to the movement to end teacher education (Kumashiro, 2010); contradictory and problematic diversity policies (White, 2016); complicit support for deprofessionalization of teacher education (Milner, 2013); and prompting rigid teacher preparation accountability regulations (Kumashiro, 2015). Despite these issues, traditional teacher education has never been a particularly welcoming and nurturing space for Teachers of Color (Chapman, 2011). In fact, since ARTs accept Teachers of Color at a higher rate than traditional teacher education programs (Hammerness & Reininger, 2008), in many ways, ARTs can create more viable entry points to the teaching profession. Yet, the implications of ARTs for community, justice, and visionaries must be more broadly investigated to better understand how they can contribute to diversifying the teacher workforce. The critical teacher development framework provides starting points for traditional teacher education and ARTs alike to begin developing recruitment and retention pipelines to attack oppressive structures that limit recruitment and retention possibilities for Teachers of Color. The ART and professional development initiatives committed to Teachers of Color in this volume suggest that critical teacher development work by ARTs is possible, despite the problematic and dispiriting efforts by some ARTs initiatives that ignore or disregard a critical teacher development stance in their design and implementation.

The types of anti-racist structures, vehicles for justice, tailored and responsive preparation, and community-based partnership and leadership identified in this volume provide a sketch of possibilities for school principals, policymakers, community organizers, teacher education programs, and district personnel to work together as key stakeholders to begin challenging and dismantling systems of oppression that restrict the recruitment and retention of Teachers of Color in schools. This work certainly requires a radical imagination. And this is not always easy because as Kelley (2002) argues,

> for obvious reasons, what we are against tends to take precedence over what we are for, which is always a more complicated and ambiguous matter. It is a testament to the legacies of oppression that opposition is so frequently contained, or that efforts to find "free space" for articulating or even realizing our dreams are so rare or marginalized. (p. 10)

This edited book project is an effort to reimagine what is possible for teacher development scholars, educators, and researchers who are committed to community, justice, and visionaries. The challenges of everyday professional survival, onslaught of oppressive educational mandates, disingenuous leaders, and a tightening of control on our time and work can stop the best of us from making such efforts. As Kelley (2002) notes,

> sometimes I think the condition of daily life, of everyday oppressions, of survival, not to mention the temporary pleasures accessible to most of us, render much of our imagination inert. We are constantly putting out fires, responding to emergencies, finding temporary refuge, all of which make it difficult to see anything other than the present. (p. 11)

Yet, we must, as Whitehead (2014) argues, look beyond what the eye can see. And the ART and professional development initiatives in this volume offer a glimpse of what is possible and challenge us in our efforts to create what we do not see. The following theory, research, and policy implications are offered for consideration based on lessons from the ART and professional development program portraits. These recommendations can be seen as a starting point for a radical imagining for teacher development. Our communities and children are depending on us to not only be dreamers, but builders.

Theory

- Identify and establish critical theoretical frameworks to anchor the mission and design of ARTs. Critical teacher development (Gist, 2017; Gist, Flores, & Claeys, 2014), critical professional development (Kohli, 2012), teacher learning orientations (Feiman-Nemser, 2011), growing critical consciousness (Valenzuela, 2016), and critical multicultural education (Sleeter, 2013) frameworks are relevant conceptual starting points to begin this work.
- In particular, with respect to the critical teacher development framework (Gist, 2017), this conceptual device needs to be applied to other ARTs to better understand the heuristic utility of the framework as both a conceptual map *and* tool to critique programs in praxis.
- Additional theoretical and conceptual work is needed that frames and defines ARTs not solely within a neoliberal political context, but also as existing on a spectrum of political possibilities that extend to creating critical liberatory education for communities of color.

Research

- Additional qualitative portraits of ARTs committed to retaining and recruiting Teachers of Color are needed.
- Comparative analysis of specific selection and employment protocols would offer a more robust picture of possibilities for developing anti-racist education structures for program entry and hiring of Teachers of Color.
- Closer analysis and investigation of pedagogy, in particular culturally responsive teacher educators (Gist, 2014b), enacted by teacher educators and community leaders of color in ARTs committed to preparing Teachers of Color would also advance our current understandings of tailored and responsive pedagogy.
- Additional research is also needed to understand the types of anti-racist program supports extended by ARTs for Teachers of Color after program completion.
- Additional research is needed to better understand the role of CBOs in the teacher development process in ARTs as justice vehicles for Teachers of Color as well as local school communities.

Praxis

- Organize a community of stakeholders who recognize, understand, and are committed to developing viable and sustainable ARTs committed to recruiting and retaining Teachers of Color.

- Identify current ARTs that are committed to anti-racist structures for Teachers of Color and conduct site visits to learn about their policies and practices.
- Examine curriculum and program design to consider who the content is geared to, what philosophies and viewpoints are dominating the preparation experiences, and who is leading most of the content delivery.
- Consider what justice vehicles are in place in the current design of the ARTs and consider changes that need to take place.
- Invite and work in partnership with local community leaders and organizations at each stage of the teacher development continuum (i.e., recruitment, preparation, induction, and retention).
- Implement inquiry action groups to explore racial justice issues within ARTs as well as local school communities.

Policy

- Develop federal, state, and district level funding policies for ARTs that explicitly support anti-racist structures for recruiting and retaining Teachers of Color.
- Reframe definitions of highly qualified teachers for ARTs to also include community and cultural connections with students.
- Adjust ARTs program evaluation systems to value and center social justice commitments to Communities and Teachers of Color.
- Require ARTs to incorporate a variety of community-based stakeholders at each stage of the teacher development continuum (i.e., recruitment, preparation, induction, retention) for Teachers of Color.

REFERENCES

Banks, J. A., & Banks, C. A. (2013). *Multicultural education: Issues and perspectives* (8th ed.). Hoboken, NJ: John Wiley & Sons.

Chapman, T. K. (2011). A critical race theory analysis of past and present institutional processes and policies in teacher education. In A. F. Ball & C. A. Tyson (Eds.), *Studying diversity in teacher education* (pp. 237–256). New York, NY: Rowman & Littlefield.

Feiman-Nemser, S. (2011). *Teachers as learners.* Cambridge, MA: Harvard Education Press.

Franklin, S. M. (2014). *After the rebellion: Black youth, social movement activism, and the post-civil rights generation.* New York, NY: NYU Press.

Gist, C. D. (2014a). *Preparing teachers of color to teach: Culturally responsive teacher education in theory and practice.* New York, NY: Palgrave Macmillan.

Gist, C. D. (2014b). The culturally responsive teacher educator. *The Teacher Educator, 49*(4), 265–283.

Gist, C.D. (2016). Culturally responsive pedagogy for teachers of color. *The New Educator*, 1–16. Retrieved from: http://dx.doi.org/10.1080/1547688X.2016.1196801

Gist, C. D. (Ed.). (2017). *Portraits of anti-racist alternative certification in the U.S.: Framing teaching for community, social justice, and visionaries.* New York, NY: Peter Lang.

Gist, C. D., Flores, B. B., & Claeys, L. (2014). A competing theory of change: Critical teacher development. In C. Sleeter, L. I. Neal, & K. K. Kumashiro (Eds.), *Addressing the demographic imperative: Recruiting, preparing, and retaining a diverse and highly effective teaching force* (pp. 19–31). New York, NY: Routledge.

Hammerness, K., & Reininger, M. (2008). Who goes into early-entry programs? In P. Grossman & S. Loeb, *Alternative routes to teaching: Mapping the new landscape of teacher education* (pp. 31–63). Cambridge, MA: Harvard Education Press.

Kelley, R. D. (2002). *Freedom dreams: The black radical imagination.* Boston, MA: Beacon Press.

Kohli, R. (2012). Racial pedagogy of the oppressed: Critical interracial dialogue for teachers of color. *Equity and Excellence in Education, 45*(1), 181–196.

Kumashiro, K. K. (2010). Seeing the bigger picture: Troubling movements to end teacher education. *Journal of Teacher Education, 61*(1–2), 56–65.

Kumashiro, K. K. (2015). *Review of proposed 2015 federal teacher preparation regulations.* Boulder, CO: National Education Policy Center. Retrieved from http://nepc.colorado.edu/thinktank/review-proposed-teacher-preparation.

Lau, K. F., Dandy, E. B., & Hoffman, L. (2007). The pathways program: A model for increasing the number of teachers of color. *Teacher Education Quarterly, 34*(3), 27–40.

Milner, R. (2013). Policy reforms and de-professionalization of teaching. Boulder, CO: National Education Policy Center. Retrieved from http://nepc.colorado.edu/publication/policy-reforms-deprofessionalization

Shroyer, G., Yahnke, S., Morales, A., Dunn, C., Lohfink, G., & Espinoza, P. (2009). Barriers and bridges to success: Factors for retention of nontraditional Mexican American students in teacher education. *Enrollment Management Journal, 3*(3), 40–73.

Sleeter, C. (2001). Preparing teachers for culturally diverse schools: Research and the overwhelming presence of whiteness. *Journal of Teacher Education, 52*(2), 94–106.

Sleeter, C. (2013). *Power, teaching, and teacher education: Confronting injustice with critical research and action.* New York, NY: Peter Lang.

Valenzuela, A. (Ed.). (2016). *Growing critically conscious teachers: A social justice curriculum for educators of Latino/a youth.* New York, NY: Teachers College Press.

White, T. (2016). Teach for America's paradoxical diversity initiative: Race, policy, and Black teacher displacement in urban public schools. *Education Policy Analysis, 24*(16), 1–37.

Whitehead, K. W. (2014). *Sparking the genius: The 2013 Woodson lecture* (pp. 29–37). Baltimore, MD: Apprentice House Publisher.

Contributor Biographies

Conra D. Gist, PhD, is an Assistant Professor in the Department of Curriculum and Instruction at the University of Arkansas and holds a Ph.D. in Urban Education at the City University of New York (CUNY) Graduate Center. Her research agenda integrates two key areas of study—racial/ethnic teacher diversity and teacher development—and takes an interdisciplinary approach to explore how culturally responsive pedagogy, critical social theories, and African American History intersect to produce just and transformative teaching and learning possibilities. She started her teaching career in Brooklyn, NY as a fourth grade teacher and currently serves as Principal Investigator for the Teacher Testimony Project, an initiative that challenges the silencing of Teachers of Color through the development and featuring of teacher testimonies. As a 2016 Spencer/National Academy of Education Postdoctoral Fellow, she is also Principal Investigator for a national study examining the experiences of Black Teachers in Grow Your Own Programs.

Rachelle Rogers-Ard, EdD, is the Executive Director, Office of Organizational Effectiveness and Culture within the Oakland Unified School District. A former teacher, Department Head, and Applied Learning Coach for ten years in Oakland, Dr. Rogers-Ard received her doctorate in Educational Leadership from Mills College in 2007 and is currently a lecturer at the University of Washington, Tacoma.

La Vonne I. Neal, PhD, is Associate Vice President for Operations at Northern Illinois University. Over the course of her academic career as Dean of the College of Education at Northern Illinois University (NIU) and Dean of the College of Education at the University of Colorado at Colorado Springs (UCCS), Neal led transformation throughout the colleges' programs. She has demonstrated experience in fostering process improvement and innovation while serving in both academic and administrative roles. Neal is a teacher educator whose work in the design and implementation of culturally responsive teaching methods has earned wide recognition both among educators and popular press. For example, her research on the correlation between African American male students' walking styles and their placement in special education courses has been featured globally in mass media. She has over 200 publications and presentations, including her most recent book—"*Diversifying the Teacher Workforce: Preparing and Retaining Highly Effective Teachers.*"

Sarah Militz-Frielink, PhD, is the LEND Coordinator and Training Director at the Center for Disabilities Sanford School of Medicine, University of South Dakota. As a coordinator for the Leadership Education in Neurodevelopmental and Related Disabilities (LEND) program, Dr. Militz-Frielink mentors and teaches graduate scholars across several disciplines in the Maternal Child Health fields. She also works in partnership with colleagues at Sinte Gleska University and Sitting Bull College to mentor and publish with Native American fellows as part of diversity training initiatives. Her most recent co-authored book—*Borders, Bras, and Battles: A Practical Guide to Mentor Undergraduate Women to Achieve Career Success*, was the recipient of a 2017 Society of Professors of Education Outstanding Book Award, Honorable Mention.

Reyes L. Quezada, PhD, is professor at the University of San Diego, in the Department of Learning and Teaching in the School Leadership and Education Sciences. His teaching and research focus are in bilingual education, equity, cultural proficiency, parent involvement, international education, inclusion, and diversity. His publications include journals and chapter contributions on international teacher education, bilingual/multicultural education, peace education, character education, home-school community involvement, teacher certification, and adventure-based education and counseling. He has extensive experience in state, national, and international boards, such as the International Council for the Education of Teachers (ICET); as past president of the California Council for Teacher Education; as vice present and board member for the American Association of Colleges for Teacher Education (AACTE); as the California representative for the Association of Teacher Educators (ATE). He is a governing board member of several journals and has been a California Commission on Teacher Credentialing-Committee on Accreditation (COA) member for the past nine years, and on the San Bernardino Equal Opportunity Commission.

Ernesto Ruiz, PhD, is a retired Superintendent of Butte County School District and past California Mini-Corps State Director.

Belinda Bustos Flores, PhD, is a Professor in the Department of Bicultural-Bilingual Studies and Associate Dean of Professional Preparation, Assessment, and Accreditation for the College of Education and Human Development at the University of Texas at San Antonio. Her research focuses on teacher development including self-concept, ethnic identity, efficacy, beliefs, teacher recruitment/retention, high stakes testing, and family cultural knowledge. Flores is founder of the Academy for Teacher Excellence.

Kate Van Winkle is the executive director of Grow Your Own Teachers Illinois. GYO is an innovative partnership of community organizations, higher education institutions, and school districts that supports parents, community members and paraprofessionals in low-income communities to become highly qualified teachers. Prior to GYO, Kate spent 15 years working on local and national social, economic and racial justice issues in a variety of roles. She is a graduate of the City University of New York School of Law.

Nicholas M. Michelli, EdD, is Presidential Professor in the Urban Education PhD program at the City University of New York's Graduate Center, where his work focuses on education policy analysis and teacher education policy. He worked in three Middle Eastern universities, among the first to admit women, to strengthen their teacher education programs. The work is reported in Teacher quality and teacher education quality: Accreditation from a global perspective (Routledge, 2017). In 2017 he conducted workshops with his PhD students on confronting racism in St. Louis and Ferguson, MO. A former dean of 25 years, he served as the first chair of the Governing Council of the National Network for Educational Renewal.

Josephine Pham is a PhD candidate in the Urban Schooling program at the University of California, Los Angeles. A former middle and high school teacher in the Bay Area, California, Josephine initially joined the Institute for a Teachers of Color (ITOC) in 2013 as a teacher and currently serves as an assistant director.

Her research interests include an examination of how change occurs through day-to-day processes and actions, particularly initiated by teachers of Color who question, challenge, and seek to transform institutional spaces towards justice for their students and themselves.

Rita Kohli, PhD, is an Assistant Professor in the Education, Society and Culture program at the Graduate School of Education at the University of California, Riverside. She is also co-founder and co-director of the Institute for Teachers of Color Committed to Racial Justice (ITOC). Using critical frameworks, Kohli's scholarship explores racialization and racism in K-12 school contexts with particular focus on teachers of Color.

Ana María Villegas, PhD, is Professor in the Department of Secondary and Special Education and Director of the Doctoral Program in Teacher Education and Teacher Development at Montclair State University. She teaches courses in teacher education policy and research, culturally responsive teaching, and sociocultural perspectives on teaching and learning. Prior to joining MSU in September 1996, she was a Senior Research Scientist with the Division of Education Policy Research of Educational Testing Service. She began her career as a teacher in the NYC Public Schools. Dr. Villegas has published widely on topics related to preparing culturally and linguistically responsive teachers as well as recruiting and preparing a diverse teaching force. Over the years she has received awards for her scholarship from the American Association of Colleges for Teacher Education, American Educational Research Association, and Educational Testing Service.

ROCHELLE BROCK & CYNTHIA DILLARD
Executive Editors

Black Studies and Critical Thinking is an interdisciplinary series which examines the intellectual traditions of and cultural contributions made by people of African descent throughout the world. Whether it is in literature, art, music, science, or academics, these contributions are vast and far-reaching. As we work to stretch the boundaries of knowledge and understanding of issues critical to the Black experience, this series offers a unique opportunity to study the social, economic, and political forces that have shaped the historic experience of Black America, and that continue to determine our future. Black Studies and Critical Thinking is positioned at the forefront of research on the Black experience, and is the source for dynamic, innovative, and creative exploration of the most vital issues facing African Americans. The series invites contributions from all disciplines but is specially suited for cultural studies, anthropology, history, sociology, literature, art, and music.

Subjects of interest include (but are not limited to):

- EDUCATION
- SOCIOLOGY
- HISTORY
- MEDIA/COMMUNICATION
- RELIGION/THEOLOGY
- WOMEN'S STUDIES
- POLICY STUDIES
- ADVERTISING
- AFRICAN AMERICAN STUDIES
- POLITICAL SCIENCE
- LGBT STUDIES

For additional information about this series or for the submission of manuscripts, please contact Dr. Brock (University of North Carolina at Greensboro) at r_brock@uncg.edu or Dr. Dillard (University of Georgia) at cdillard@uga.com.

To order other books in this series, please contact our Customer Service Department:

(800) 770-LANG (within the U.S.)
(212) 647-7706 (outside the U.S.)
(212) 647-7707 FAX

Or browse online by series at www.peterlang.com.